MOVERS AND SHAKERS

Scharada Dubey is a writer, internet consultant and Tarot practitioner. She has won several writing awards and her books for children include the travelogues *Footloose on the West Coast, Malwa on My Mind* and *A Necessary Journey.*

MOVERS AND SHAKERS
Prime Ministers of India 1947 to 2009

Scharada Dubey

Westland Ltd

westland ltd.

61, Silverline Building, Alapakkam Main Road, Maduravoyal,
Chennai 600 095
93, 1st Floor, Sham Lal Road, Daryaganj, New Delhi 110 002

Frist published by westland ltd 2009

10 9 8 7 6 5 4 3 2 1

ISBN: 978-81-89975-54-8

Illustrations: Rahul Krishnan

Typeset in RotisSemiSans by Mindways Design, New Delhi

Contents

Introduction

The popular head of the Indian government, the prime minister is vital to the shape and direction of our development and progress. In our sixty-odd year history as an independent nation, we have had comparatively few prime ministers. This fact is witness to the stability of Indian democracy, even as it underscores the strong mandate enjoyed by long-serving prime ministers, such as our first prime minister – Jawaharlal Nehru.

No study of India and its history can be complete without a look at the personalities that emerged at different periods of crisis, the quality of their leadership and the compelling circumstances that affected their decision-making. While our prime ministers may be few, their personal history, and the manner in which this impacted the history of our country, bears investigation.

This book is an attempt to bridge the gap between contemporary readers and those of our leaders who may have passed into the pages of history, but whose contribution is visible at different levels of society today. I am grateful to Westland Ltd for giving me this assignment and to Deepthi Talwar for her consistent support during the entire project. I hope that readers, young and old, will find these profiles an absorbing read that unravels several chapters from our contemporary history.

Scharada Dubey

Jawaharlal Nehru (1889–1964)

India's First Prime Minister
Jawaharlal Nehru

Term of Office: 15 August 1947–27 May 1964

Perhaps no other prime minister could be said to embody the very idea of India as successfully as the nation's first prime minister, Jawaharlal Nehru. He is often the favourite whipping boy of the Hindutva-espousing nationalist parties, because he represented an inclusive Indianness that they belittle as 'pseudo-secularism'. There is no denying that Nehru was a man with a big vision for India, a patriot who helped build many of the institutions and practices that provided a foundation for our country.

A participant in the struggle for Indian independence and Mahatma Gandhi's trusted lieutenant, Nehru became the first prime minister of independent India. He was a nationalist whose ideas of social reform had been shaped by exposure to Western ideas of equality, justice and liberty as much as by the guidance and wisdom of Mahatma Gandhi. Born into a wealthy family on 14 November 1889 at Allahabad, Nehru was the son of Motilal Nehru, a rich and distinguished lawyer. Motilal Nehru's Kashmiri Brahmin family had moved to Allahabad from Kashmir some generations before Jawaharlal was born. Motilal was a member of the Indian National Congress, and was married to Swaroop Rani.

His father's patriotic leanings and involvement with the Congress meant that Jawaharlal was exposed to discussion and debate about India's independence from a very early age. In later years, father and son would differ in their approach to India's freedom. Motilal, like several others in the Congress leadership, was ready for India to be given dominion status within the British Empire. Jawaharlal, fighting shoulder to shoulder with Mahatma Gandhi, was committed to fighting for total independence.

Jawaharlal grew up in the large, rambling family home called Anand Bhavan in Allahabad. The house, garden and stables were the broad territory for him to lead a virtually solitary childhood because his three sisters were all much younger than him. A series of English governesses and tutors were employed to teach Jawaharlal. He was very polite and well behaved, and brought up in the tradition of Western manners, dress and language. However, he was also provided a grounding in Indian culture through a special tutor who taught him Hindi and Sanskrit.

Books took the place of friends and playmates. Jawaharlal read voraciously and was familiar with the works of Walter Scott, Charles Dickens, Thackeray, H.G. Wells and Mark Twain, as well as philosophical and political writers like John Stuart Mill, Gladstone, John Morley, Bertrand Russell and Bernard Shaw. This love of letters is what shaped his later career as a powerful orator, writer and thinker.

Jawaharlal's parents sent him to study in England at the age of fifteen. He first attended school at Harrow, and then university at Cambridge, finally studying to become a barrister at the Inner Temple in London. He returned to India in 1912, and began practising law at the Allahabad high court.

His long stay in England was not marked by scholastic rigour so much as the fine pursuits of any fashionable young English gentleman. He spent time playing tennis, rowing and some mild forms of gambling. His shyness proved to be something of a handicap in these years. A member of the Cambridge debating team, he often had to pay fines for not speaking during the entire term!

Back from abroad, Nehru was awakened to the struggle for Indian independence by a series of events. One was the issue of Annie Besant's imprisonment in 1917; another was the Jallianwalla Bagh massacre in 1919, when four hundred Indians were shot on the orders of a British officer. In 1920 he first encountered at very close quarters the extreme poverty of millions of his countrymen. He was on a trip to the rural areas around Allahabad, when he saw first-hand how millions of his countrymen lived, and what freedom meant to them. Touring the rural districts near Allahabad with some colleagues, he spent three days in remote areas far from railway stations, or good roads. For the first time, he saw first-hand how much the ideal of freedom from British rule had gripped the imagination of even the poorest people. Villagers came running out of their fields and houses to greet the young men from the city. Their tattered clothes and humble dwellings brought home to Jawaharlal the overwhelming poverty prevalent in large parts of India. But it also showed him how his countrymen and women expected freedom from the British to provide the miracle that would end their misery. Deeply affected by the scenes he witnessed in rural India. Nehru was encouraged by the fact that the crowds seemed to receive him with great affection. This connection with the people remained with him all through his subsequent years as a freedom-fighter, and later, prime minister of independent India.

This moving encounter with the rural masses strengthened Nehru's commitment to fight for the poorest and most disadvantaged. He had embraced Fabian socialism as an ideal in his student days in England; now his socialism began to be much more firmly grounded in the real-life conditions in India.

Nehru first met Mahatma Gandhi in 1916. At first, what struck Nehru was how, in spite of having had an education quite similar to his own, Gandhi remained essentially Indian in everything he did. Nehru, on the other hand, had once described himself while at Cambridge as being more an Englishman than an Indian in his likes and dislikes. Gandhi's approach, that Britain could be resisted without fear or hate, attracted Nehru. After he plunged into the Non-Cooperation Movement launched by Mahatma Gandhi in 1920, Nehru began to be primarily Indian in lifestyle, approach and expression. His daily routine included reading from the *Bhagavad Gita*, and yoga. His dress and attire became kurtas, sherwanis and churidars, and the cap that became a distinguishing feature and a symbol of Congressmen thereafter.

The year Nehru met Gandhi, his parents arranged his marriage with Kamala Kaul, a young Kashmiri woman brought up in an orthodox Kashmiri Brahmin family. The couple had one daughter – Indira Priyadarshini, who was born in November 1917. Nehru's taking to Indian ways of dress and speech, and following Mahatma Gandhi's values of simple living, were welcomed by his wife. She was a woman firmly grounded in Indian ways, unlike Nehru's sisters, who were much more influenced by Western manners of speech and dress. One of Nehru's sisters, Vijaya Lakshmi Pandit, later became the first woman president of the UN General Assembly.

In 1921, Nehru went to prison for the first time. Over the next twenty-four years, as the struggle for independence gathered momentum, Nehru would go on to serve another eight periods in jail. In 1923 he became general secretary of the Congress, and this appointment was given to him again in 1927. His thinking was shaped to no mean extent by his tour of Europe and the erstwhile Soviet Union in 1926–27. It was during this visit that he met many socialist leaders and saw the reconstruction of a country and society on the basis of socialism. This convinced him about the need for an economic revolution, which would free India from an over-dependence on agriculture.

When the Simon Commission was set up by the British to decide the type of constitution or the kind of independence that India should obtain for itself, Nehru resisted the idea of dominion status. At the Congress session in Calcutta in December 1928, he and Subhash Chandra Bose put forward the claim for complete independence as the Congress objective. In the following year, he was elected president of the Indian National Congress at the Lahore session. Here, he gave the call for purna swaraj or complete independence.

As the clock struck midnight on the night of 31 December 1929, he led a solemn procession on the banks of the Ravi river and raised India's national flag.

Nehru attracted the country's intellectuals and youth to the Congress movement. After Motilal Nehru died in 1931, Jawaharlal became closer to Mahatma Gandhi, even though he was not announced as his political heir till 1942. In the 1936–37 election campaign for the provincial legislatures under the Government of India Act of 1935, Nehru proved to be the principal vote-getter for the Congress.

Nehru's imprisonment during the Quit India Movement of 1942 proved to be his longest term in prison. He emerged in 1945 and spent the next two years in painful negotiations with Jinnah's Muslim League – a process that ultimately ended with the partition of India and the emergence of two independent countries, India and Pakistan.

As prime minister of independent India from 1947 till his death in 1964, Nehru greatly impacted the thinking and development of his people and country. He adapted modern values to Indian conditions. One of his greatest achievements was his emphasis on secularism and on the basic unity of India, despite its racial, religious and linguistic diversity. He encouraged the scientific temper and inspired people to have a concern for the poor and respect for democratic values. He enabled the reform of the ancient Hindu civil code that finally entitled Hindu widows to enjoy equality with men in matters of inheritance and property. As prime minister of a nation that had long been subjugated by foreign rule, he considered it his first task to move the country towards rapid technical and industrial advances and self-sufficiency in agriculture and industry.

Nehru enjoyed the reputation of a statesman who was an articulate spokesman for the cause of non-alignment in the international arena. He made India a country to reckon with by adopting the policy of non-alignment from the then two superpowers of the world, America and Russia. However, this reputation was dented in October 1956, when India did not vote with other nations condemning the Soviet invasion of Hungary. He was challenged all through his term as prime minister by the problem of Kashmir, and India made several adjustments along the Line of Control in order to improve prospects of peace with Pakistan. However, it was the Chinese aggression of 1962, a country with which Nehru had been attempting to have friendly ties, which shattered his peace of mind and led to the deterioration of his health.

Nehru's speeches are remembered and recited by children for their historic and stirring content. He is particularly known for his 'Tryst with Destiny' or 'Freedom at Midnight' speech and his books, which include *Glimpses of World History and Discovery of India.* He was especially approachable to children, whom he dearly loved. It is for this reason that children called him 'Chacha Nehru' or Uncle Nehru, and his birthday, 14 November, is still celebrated as 'Children's Day' across the country.

Nehru's modern political and economic outlook, his proud articulation of being a free Indian on the world stage, and his respect for science and technology helped shape India's development in the years after independence. Many consider Gandhi to be India's liberator, and Nehru its moderniser. During his seventeen years in office, the four pillars of Nehru's domestic policies were democracy, socialism, unity and secularism. His name and character stand for these values even today.

Gulzari Lal Nanda (1898–1998)

Twice Interim Prime Minister
Gulzari Lal Nanda

Terms of Office: 27 May 1964–9 June 1964,
11 January 1966–24 January 1966

India's history has two instances when a prime minister died in office and an acting prime minister was appointed. Both these instances happened in the 1960s, both had Gulzari Lal Nanda appointed as caretaker prime minister, and the period of both these terms was thirteen days.

The first time Nanda took over as interim prime minister was following the death of Jawaharlal Nehru on 27 May 1964. The second was following the death of Lal Bahadur Shastri in 1966. While these two thirteen-day terms were largely uneventful, they were important because India was vulnerable in both those periods – the first followed a war with China in 1962 and the second, a war with Pakistan in 1965.

Who was the man twice trusted at the country's helm, who did not draw any further mileage from his historic appointments?

Nanda was an economist and a labour expert who lived by Gandhian values. He was born on 4 July 1898, in Sialkot, a town that passed into Pakistan following the partition of Punjab. He studied at Lahore, Agra and Allahabad, working as a research scholar on labour problems at the University of Allahabad from 1920 to 1921. He later became a professor of economics at the National College, Bombay, in 1921, and joined the struggle for independence through the Non-Cooperation Movement in that same year. He worked at the Ahmedabad Textile Labour Association from 1922 to 1946, serving as its secretary in 1922. He was twice imprisoned by the British for his part in the freedom struggle, in 1932, and again from 1942 to 1944 for his participation in the Quit India Movement.

Nanda was elected to the Bombay Legislative Assembly in 1937 and appointed parliamentary secretary, Labour and Excise, to the government of Bombay from 1937 to 1939. He later also served as Labour minister of the Bombay government from 1946 to 1950, and played an important role in building and organising the Indian National Trade Union Congress or INTUC. He later served as the president of INTUC as well.

It was these positions wherein he was deeply engaged with the problems of labour in the country that led to Nanda going abroad on several occasions to attend conferences on labour issues. He went to Geneva in 1947 as a representative of the Government of India, to the International Labour Conference. He was an active member of the Freedom of Association Committee appointed by the Conference, and visited Sweden, France, Switzerland, Belgium and England to study labour and housing conditions in those countries.

Nanda's expertise was called upon to contribute to the Planning Commission, the Central body that was set up under Jawaharlal Nehru's leadership to provide Five Year plans for India's economic progress. He joined the Commission in March 1950 as its vice-chairman. In September 1951 he began work as the minister for Planning in the Union government. He also had charge of the portfolios of Irrigation and Power. In the general elections of 1952, he won from Bombay and entered the Lok Sabha, again being given the ministerial portfolios of Planning, Irrigation and Power.

Gulzari Lal Nanda's contributions to administration and planning continued after his re-election to the Lok Sabha in 1957. He was then appointed Union minister for Labour and Employment and Planning. Later, he served as deputy chairman of the Planning Commission. In the next general elections in 1962, he was re-elected to the Lok Sabha from Sabarkantha in Gujarat. Within the Congress party, he initiated the Congress Forum for Socialist Action in 1962, at a time when he was Union minister for Labour and Employment. From 1963 to 1966 he served as the minister for Home Affairs, a significant portfolio that capped his political career.

Nanda lived and worked by Mahatma Gandhi's principles. He lived to be a centenarian, passing away in 1998, a year after he was honoured by the Government of India with its highest civilian honour, the Bharat Ratna.

Lal Bahadur Shastri (1904–1966)

Brave and Beloved Prime Minister
Lal Bahadur Shastri

Term of Office: 9 June 1964–11 January 1966

The history of independent India has seen several chapters when the country has been deprived of the courage, wisdom and leadership of a particular individual by their untimely death. The premature death of Lal Bahadur Shastri, the second prime minister of our country, ranks as one of the biggest losses to India.

Lal Bahadur Shastri, who shared a birthday with Mahatma Gandhi, was born on 2 October 1904 at Mughalsarai, the town made famous as an important railway junction by the British, in Uttar Pradesh. His father, Sharada Prasad, was a school teacher who later became a clerk in the revenue office at Allahabad. The big tragedy the family faced was Sharada Prasad's death when

Lal Bahadur was a mere infant. This meant that his mother, Ramdulari Devi, had to bring up Lal Bahadur and his two sisters at her father's house.

Several incidents from Lal Bahadur's childhood indicate the hardships he had to undergo due to the financial constraints imposed by his father's death. On one occasion, he was reprimanded by a teacher at school for wearing wet clothes. Receiving a sharp rap from a cane for this offence, he remained quiet. However, under the teacher's insistent questioning as to why his clothes were wet when it was not even raining, he replied that he had swum across the river Ganga in order to reach school. The one paise cost of the boat ride across the river was too much for his family to bear at that time. The teacher was filled with shame, and was struck by the little boy's devotion to school and studying.

On another occasion, when he was six years old, he accompanied some friends on the way back from school into an orchard. He stood below the trees while his friends plucked mangoes. But when the gardener in charge of the orchard came there, it was Lal Bahadur whom he caught, and began scolding and beating. Pleading with the gardener to let him go, Lal Bahadur asked him to forgive him, as he was a fatherless child. What he had not bargained for was the gardener's response, which left a deep impression on his psyche. 'Because you don't have a father to guide you, it is all the more important for you to behave better than these rascals,' said the gardener.

Lal Bahadur's participation in India's freedom struggle began when he was a mere teenager. He stayed at his grandfather's house till he was ten years old, by which time he had passed the sixth standard examination. He then went to Varanasi to study further. He was only seventeen years old when Mahatma Gandhi launched the Non-Cooperation Movement against the British government in 1921. Responding to Mahatma Gandhi's call to the youth to boycott government schools and colleges, offices and courts and to sacrifice everything for the sake of freedom, Shastri quit school against the advice of his mother and relatives. He was arrested at this time for his involvement in the movement, but let off by the British authorities as he was so young. His diminutive stature must have made him appear even younger.

Having boycotted the education offered by the British government, Lal Bahadur joined the

Kashi Vidya Peeth and studied philosophy for four years. He earned the honorific 'Shastri' in 1926, signifying great learning. He completed his studies at Kashi Vidya Peeth, and joined The Servants of the People Society, which Lala Lajpat Rai had started in 1921. This society trained youths who wanted to dedicate their lives to the service of their countrymen. It was during this period, in 1927, that Shastri married Lalita Devi. Their wedding was a study in simplicity. A small ceremony saw the bride being sent off with her husband and the dowry her family gave the couple was a spinning wheel and a few yards of khadi cloth.

Meanwhile, Shastri's commitment to the freedom struggle was deepening. When Gandhi called for the Civil Disobedience Movement in 1930, Shastri exhorted people not to pay land revenue and taxes to the government. He was arrested and jailed for two-and-a-half years for this. He used the time in jail to continue his education, becoming familiar with the works of Western philosophers, revolutionaries and social reformers.

The Congress launched its 'individual satyagraha' movement in 1940 to intensify the demand for independence. Shastri was arrested again and jailed for a year. He was an active participant in the 1942 Quit India Movement, and went underground, but was later arrested. He was released in 1945 along with other senior leaders.

A fresh phase of his political life began at this point. In 1946, during the provincial elections, his hard work, administrative ability and organisational skills were noticed by Pandit Govind Ballabh Pant. When Pant became the chief minister of Uttar Pradesh, he appointed Shastri as his parliamentary secretary. In 1947 India became independent and Shastri became the minister of Police and Transport in Pant's United Provinces, or Uttar Pradesh, government.

The first general elections after independence were held with Shastri occupying the post of general secretary of the Congress party. Not surprisingly, the Congress returned to power with a huge majority. With his stature rising constantly within the organisation of the Congress, Jawaharlal Nehru appointed Shastri as his Railways and Transport minister in the Central Cabinet in 1952. This appointment benefited Indians forever because of Shastri's initiative in providing more facilities to travellers in third class compartments; he bridged the vast difference between first and third class travel. In an example of moral responsibility and integrity rarely seen today, Shastri resigned as minister of Railways in 1956, after a railway accident. Although Nehru tried to persuade him to reconsider, he refused to back down from his stand. By his uncompromising and courageous action, Shastri was setting new standards of morality in public life.

In 1957, the Congress returned to power, and Shastri was given the portfolio of Transport and Communications. He later also served as the minister for Commerce and Industry. A significant role was played by him in the 1962 war with China. He inspired the people to contribute to the war effort through stirring acts of personal sacrifice. At a time when the Indian economy could ill afford a war, ordinary citizens contributed with their belongings and jewellery, to raise resources for our soldiers. By then, he had become the Home minister and was in charge of internal security during the war.

Shastri's popularity, both within and outside the Congress, was evident to everyone. This was the reason why he was unanimously elected as the prime minister of India after the death of Jawaharlal Nehru in 1964. Taking up the challenge of leading India at the time was no easy task. There was an acute shortage of food and a war with Pakistan appeared imminent. Sure enough, in 1965, Pakistan attacked India to begin the Indo-Pak war of 1965. It was in this difficult period that Shastri underlined the importance of farmers and soldiers for the country by coining the slogan 'Jai jawan, Jai kisan' (Hail the soldier! Hail the farmer!).

Shastri was such a mild-mannered man that it was difficult to believe how his dynamic leadership helped to lead and inspire India through a war, and food shortage. Pakistan lost this war and Shastri's leadership began to be recognised all over the world.

It was evident that Shastri, whose childhood and youth had been spent in conditions very different from those of Jawaharlal Nehru, had a very good idea of the aspirations and needs of the common people, and could grow into a leader who would lead India towards development with a human face. Unfortunately, our country never had the opportunity to experience this leadership much beyond the 1965 Indo-Pak war. In January

1966, a historic meeting was arranged at Tashkent in Russia between India and Pakistan. This meeting, brought about through Russia's efforts, was held between Shastri and Ayub Khan, then president of Pakistan. A joint declaration was signed in Tashkent under Russian mediation in which India agreed to return to Pakistan all the territories it had occupied during the war of 1965. This joint declaration was signed on 10 January 1966. Tragically, that same night, Shastri died of a heart attack.

Grieving Indians found it hard to come to terms with the death of their beloved Shastri at a foreign location and conspiracy theories abounded at the time. Many suggested that Shastri had been killed by the Russians, the Pakistanis or both.

In many ways, the premature death of Shastri gave the political history of India a very regrettable twist from which it never fully recovered. This small-built man was truly a very tall leader of men.

Indira Gandhi (1917–1984)

First Woman Prime Minister
Indira Gandhi

Terms of Office: 24 January 1966–24 March 1977; 14 January 1980–31 October 1984

Jawaharlal Nehru held the office of prime minister for almost seventeen years before his death in 1964. When he died, few could have imagined that there would be another prime minister who would rival his long tenure, and that person would be his daughter. Ever since she was made prime minister by a syndicate of top Congress leaders in 1966 following the death of Lal Bahadur Shastri, Indira Gandhi ruled India as if she had been born for the job. She never looked back, managing to regain power after an electoral defeat and political humiliation.

There is no doubt that Indira Gandhi was one of the country's most significant leaders in the seventies and eighties — two decades when India was evolving from a poor, developing country into an important player on the world stage. Yet, while her importance for India is uncontested, Indira Gandhi's style of functioning and leadership has been criticised as being dictatorial. Her personal hold over the Congress party and the culture of sycophancy that prevailed in her ministerial Cabinet had a very harmful effect on the political atmosphere of the country as a whole.

Indira Gandhi's childhood wasn't easy. Her birth, on 19 November 1917, was reportedly a disappointment to her grandfather Motilal Nehru and many others in her paternal family, who had hoped for a son to follow in Nehru's footsteps. Indira's mother, Kamala Nehru, was a frail and sickly woman who was allegedly treated none too kindly by her sisters-in-law. As a child Indira resented their treatment of her mother, but was unable to do anything about it. Her father's long absences from home as a Congress freedom fighter, or because he was in prison, and her mother's poor health made life very difficult for Indira. Undoubtedly, this childhood in Anand Bhavan at Allahabad, the palatial home that was an elaborate replica of an English country home, surrounded by forest-like gardens, and with the presence of almost a hundred people in the house, including servants, had a lot to do with the shaping of Indira's character. But her silent observation of her childhood tormentors actually taught her a great deal about human nature — data she used to good effect as a politician in later years.

Indira Gandhi escaped the oppressive atmosphere of her family home when she went away to study — first at the Ecole Nouvelle in Bex, Switzerland, then the Ecole Internationale, Geneva, Pupils' Own School, Poona and Bombay, Badminton School, Bristol, Vishwa Bharati, Shantiniketan and finally Somerville College, Oxford.

Very early in life, Indira became aware of two important and defining influences in her life — her father and Mahatma Gandhi — and after the completion of her education in 1938, she joined the Indian National Congress party and became active in the freedom movement. While she was still a child she had founded the Bal Charkha Sangh, and in 1930, the Vanar Sena — the children's wing of the Congress — to help the party during the Non-Cooperation Movement.

Indira Nehru married Feroze Gandhi, a Parsi lawyer active in the Congress party, on 26 March

1942 and the couple had two sons, Rajiv and Sanjay, both of whom would play a role in India's politics and history. Shortly after they were married, Indira and Feroze were arrested by the British and spent little over a year in prison. After independence in 1947, when her father took over as India's first prime minister, Indira Gandhi became his official hostess. She occupied a number of important posts in the Congress party from 1955 till the time of her death. She was a member of the Congress Working Committee in 1955; member, Central Parliamentary Board of Congress, 1958; president, All India Youth Congress, and Women's Department AICC 1956; president, Indian National Congress, 1959–60 and from January 1978 till her death in 1984.

None of the senior Congress leaders, known as the 'Syndicate' or 'Congress Caucus', who chose the young daughter of Jawaharlal Nehru to take over as prime minister after Shastri's death had any inkling as to what the future would hold. Indira's rise to the prime minister's post was opposed by Morarji Desai, then one of the most senior leaders within the Congress. Desai's objections were overcome by making him deputy prime minister. But his initial opposition was enough to have marked him forever in Indira's memory as a dangerous rival.

Indira, propelled from her post as minister for Information and Broadcasting in Shastri's Cabinet to that of prime minister after his death, continued in the post after the general elections of 1967, in which the Congress won a majority. However, the short time she had been prime minister in the months before the election had been full of challenges: there were Mizo tribal uprisings in the Northeast; food shortages across the country that had been nearly constant since 1961; labour unrest that had engulfed the state of West Bengal; the effects of a devaluation in the rupee; and agitation in Punjab for linguistic and religious separatism.

Some of these crises and the growing dissatisfaction among the people led to a reduced majority for the Congress in Parliament, and non-Congress governments were formed in Bihar, Kerala, Orissa, Madras, Punjab and West Bengal. In the politically significant state of Uttar Pradesh, a Congress-led coalition government collapsed, and Rajasthan was brought under President's Rule because of political instability there. From day one of her new job as prime minister, Indira

Gandhi had to be on her toes. She tackled the mammoth challenge of poverty with a vigorous policy of land reform and placed a ceiling on personal income, private property, and corporate profits. In 1969 she nationalised the major banks, a bold step that brought her many detractors within her own party.

But the biggest challenge to her authority was yet to come. She had taken away the Finance portfolio from Morarji Desai and sidelined him in keeping with the uneasy relationship they shared. In November 1969 the hostility between these two leaders expressed itself with a split in the Congress party. The two factions that emerged were the Congress (O), for Organisation, led by Morarji Desai, and the Congress (R), for Requisition, led by Indira Gandhi. Later this became the Congress (I), standing for Indira. In 1969, Indira overcame the challenge put up by Desai's loyalists by winning over more legislators and important leaders to her side, and continued as prime minister with support from the Communists, Sikhs, and regional parties.

The 1971 general election was bitterly fought by both factions of the Congress and other opposition parties. Indira Gandhi fought under the slogan 'Garibi Hatao' or 'Eliminate Poverty', which struck an instant chord with millions of Indians. In contrast, the Morarji Desai faction was keeping 'Indira Hatao' or 'Eliminate Indira', as their main objective, and this negative tactic did not fare well with the people.

Indira Gandhi's faction, the Congress (R), gained a large majority in Parliament, decisively pushing the Congress (O) into obscurity. That same year, India's decisive victory in the Indo-Pak war of December 1971, and the repatriation of nearly a crore of refugees from Bangladesh to their country, brought about a surge in Indira's popularity.

Unfortunately, it seemed as if the more absolute Indira's hold over the prime minister's post was, the less tolerant she was of criticism, or any form of opposition. She developed a pattern of nominating and removing state chief ministers whenever she wished, and also had frequent Cabinet reshuffles. Faced with such a whimsical style of functioning, party members began to compete with each other in parading their loyalty to Indira. Meanwhile, a twenty-year treaty of peace, friendship, and cooperation with the Soviet Union consolidated India's position in an international arena dominated by the Cold War, and underlined Indira's personal stature on the global scene.

However, difficult times were in store, as the enormous cost of the 1971 war created a deep economic crisis. This was aggravated by the costs of managing the refugees, crop failures in 1972 and 1973, skyrocketing world oil prices in 1973–74, and an overall drop in the nation's industrial output despite a surplus of scientifically and technically trained personnel. Economic recovery seemed distant in spite of a loan from the International Monetary Fund in 1974.

Indira Gandhi briefly recovered some ground with India's first nuclear test, conducted at Pokhran on 18 May 1974, which brought her leadership domestic accolades even as it met with disapproval from the elite group of nuclear-armed countries such as the US. They saw this as a dangerous development for South Asia, because of the history of frequent Indo-Pak conflicts.

However, in the same year, Indira Gandhi's prime ministerial leadership came under further challenge from the long-running railways strike led by political activist George Fernandes. There was also a national civil disobedience movement called Total Revolution building up under the call of freedom fighter and political leader Jayaprakash Narayan. Further worries were added by the defeat of her party in Gujarat by a coalition of parties calling itself the Janata Morcha (People's Front); a no-confidence motion in Parliament backed by all parties; and, most importantly, a judgement of the Allahabad high court in 1975 that held her 1971 election as invalid and debarred her from facing elections or occupying the prime minister's chair for six years.

Indira Gandhi was faced with a critical decision: she could either respect the judicial decision and bow out of office, letting someone else take over the reins of the country, or she could hold on to power, ignoring the strictures of the court. She chose the latter.

On 25 June 1975, President Fakhruddin Ali Ahmed declared a state of Emergency and the government suspended civil rights. This provision of the Constitution had earlier only been invoked during wartime. But now, Indira cited the growing opposition to her within the country as a threat to the security of the country, and had the Emergency declared. Thousands of her political opponents were jailed across the country.

Amendments to the Constitution that cleared Indira Gandhi of any wrongdoing in her election case, and the imposition of President's Rule in Gujarat and Tamil Nadu, where anti-Indira parties ruled, were among the many destructive decisions she took in this period, with all opposition silenced and jailed.

At this time, her younger son, Sanjay Gandhi, became her trusted confidante and an enthusiastic advocate of the Emergency. He unleashed a series of measures, such as forced sterilisation of the poor as a means of birth control, the razing of slums and hutments in Delhi in the name of beautification, and other actions that led to the Emergency being referred to as the Reign of Terror.

Confident that she would be able to overcome all her opponents, many of whom had spent nearly two years in prison, Indira Gandhi called off the Emergency on 18 January 1977, announced the next general election in March and released her opponents from prison.

Elections were only two months away, yet, on being released from prison, Jayaprakash Narayan and Morarji Desai brought together members from all parties who had been opposed to Indira Gandhi and formed the Janata Party so they could fight the elections on a united platform. There was widespread anger and resentment against Indira and Sanjay Gandhi for the excesses that had been committed during the Emergency. The voters of India, committed to democracy and shrewdly suspicious of what smacked of dictatorship, roundly defeated the Congress (I) and voted in the Janata Party to power.

Morarji Desai became India's fourth prime minister. However, he could be at the helm for only two years, from 1977 to 1979, because factionalism and internal competition between different prime ministerial aspirants made it inherently unstable. Desai's government was followed by Charan Singh's, which was similarly short-lived. In January 1980, fresh mid-term elections were announced, and people were faced with a dilemma. While the Congress (I) and Indira had proved harmful and dictatorial, their replacement, the Janata Party, had proved extremely disappointing in terms of the calibre of its leadership, and its inability to solve the real problems of people. Indira Gandhi and her party thus regained power, with Sanjay Gandhi being elected to the Lok Sabha.

This stint of Indira Gandhi's rule was marred by tragedy, beginning with Sanjay's death in June

1980 in an air crash. The economy was sluggish and could not show the industrial growth that had been possible during the Emergency. Reactionary movements for separate states in Punjab and by the All Assam Students Union in Assam, proved difficult to manage. The Soviet occupation of Afghanistan in December 1979 was a point of recurring diplomatic worry.

Increasingly, Indira Gandhi began to use the services of the armed forces in dealing with violent demonstrations and movements within the country. In May 1984, armed Sikh extremists occupied the Golden Temple in Amritsar. Indira Gandhi had the extremists flushed out of the shrine in early June with Operation Bluestar, a bloody battle in which many soldiers, extremists and civilians were killed or injured. The use of soldiers within the sanctum sanctorum of the Golden Temple caused such fierce resentment among the Sikh community that Indira Gandhi was assassinated by her Sikh bodyguards on 31 October 1984.

Following the news of Indira Gandhi's assassination, violent anti-Sikh riots rocked Delhi and other parts of India, in which thousands of Sikhs were killed, their homes looted and businesses destroyed. Several Congress leaders were later implicated in these riots. It was a saddening farewell for someone who had ruled the country for so long and through so many crises.

While Indira Gandhi's leadership was marked by personal flaws, she never lacked courage, and her stewardship of India on the world stage and particularly within the Non-Aligned Movement earned worldwide respect. This shy and reserved girl from Anand Bhavan went on to have Honorary doctoral degrees conferred on her by a host of universities such as El Salvador of Buenos Aires, Waseda of Tokyo, Moscow State, Oxford, Charles of Prague, Mauritius, Baghdad and the USSR apart from many in India. She received the Bharat Ratna in 1972, the Mexican Academy Award for Liberation of Bangladesh in 1972; the Mothers' Award, USA, in 1953; the Isabella d'Este Award of Italy for outstanding work in diplomacy; Yale University's Howland Memorial Prize for two consecutive years in 1967 and 1968. In the same years, Indira Gandhi was the woman the French most admired according to a poll by the French Institute of Public Opinion. A special Gallup Poll Survey in USA in 1971 showed her to be the most admired person of the world.

Many facets of Indira Gandhi's personality have been brought out by different biographers. Her own writings, letters and speeches also speak of the challenges she faced. However, in some respects she will always remain an enigma. Just when one finds something to dislike about her, a streak of great goodness is discovered. Just when you begin to think she was Durga Mata for India, you see her ruthless and amoral side. Her life and times present no easy or simple evaluation.

Morarji Desai (1896–1995)

Guided by Principles
Morarji Desai

Term of Office: 24 March 1977–28 July 1979

The picture of spare austerity and physical fitness, one prime minister of India went on to achieve remarkable longevity. He died at the age of ninety-nine, sixteen years after resigning from office as prime minister. This upright and principled freedom fighter presided over a tumultuous period of government formation and dissolution, political alignments and infighting. He was Morarji Ranchhodji Desai, known to many of his followers and admirers as Morarji Bhai.

Morarji Desai was born on 29 February 1896 in Bhadeli village, in the Valsad district of Gujarat. The son of a school teacher, he studied at St Busar High School, and later attended Wilson College in Mumbai for his matriculation.

In 1911, he married Gujraben and began working in the Civil Service of the then Bombay Province in 1918, where he served as a deputy collector for twelve years.

A career in administration was considered a great privilege, but its lure was not enough to keep Desai out of the freedom struggle. He resigned from the Civil Service post under the British and plunged into the struggle for India's independence in 1930. Becoming active in the Indian National Congress, he was a member of the All India Congress Committee from 1931 and became the secretary of the Gujarat Pradesh Congress Committee. In 1937, the first Congress government took office in Bombay Province, led by B.G. Kher, and Desai was appointed its minister for Revenue, Agriculture, Forest and Cooperatives.

Two years later, in 1939, the British government decided to engage India in the Second World War in utter disregard of the opinions of ordinary Indians. Agitated by this arbitrary decision, the entire B.G. Kher-led ministry resigned in protest. Following this, Desai's involvement in the freedom struggle intensified, and he was arrested for participating in the non-violent form of protest against the

British government made famous by Mahatma Gandhi as satyagraha. He was freed in October 1941, only to be re-arrested in August 1942 for participating in the Quit India Movement. When he was released from jail in 1945, Desai stood for elections to the state Assemblies in 1946, and became the minister for Home and Revenue in Bombay Province when the new government was sworn in. This was a period of intense reform in land revenue, with demands for 'land to the tiller' and provisions for the security of tenancy rights. The reforms initiated by Desaid made him a very popular leader and were the chief reason for his becoming the chief minister of Bombay Province in 1952.

Desai was known as a chief minister who upheld principles and wielded authority with a tough and impartial stance. He enjoyed a distinguished few years in power in this office before being appointed as Union Cabinet minister for Commerce and Industry on 14 November 1956. He was given the Finance portfolio on 22 March 1958. Desai's influence over developments in Bombay Province continued with his presence at the Centre. The year 1960 saw the emergence of Marathi linguistic movements in Bombay, calling for the creation of a separate linguistic state. At one of the demonstrations, organised by the Samyukta Maharashtra Samiti, Desai instructed the Bombay government to fire into the crowd, which led to the deaths of 105 demonstrators. The public outrage that followed this incident reached the government at the Centre and eventually led to the formation of the present state of Maharashtra.

Desai was a Gandhian, but a conservative only in social terms. While he had been Home minister of Bombay Province, Desai had come down heavily on portrayals of what he perceived was indecent in films and theatre. However, he was favourable to business and free enterprise. In this, his way of thinking differed from Prime Minister Jawaharlal Nehru's socialist policies; and, as he began to make his presence felt among the leadership of the Congress, these differences led to Desai's being overlooked for the position of a possible successor to Nehru. Instead, the mantle fell on Lal Bahadur Shastri, a man who was more in the socialist mould than Desai. Not seeing this as a negative development, as Shastri was a very able and popular person, Desai instead began to concentrate on party matters and strengthening the Congress cadre.

Shastri persuaded Desai to become chairman of the Administrative Reforms Commission, set up to restructure the administrative system. Desai's long and varied experience in administration, from British times to independent India, made him ideally suited to this task.

Shastri's premature death plunged the country and the Congress party into crisis. When Indira Gandhi, then a political novice, took charge as prime minister in 1967, Desai joined her Cabinet as deputy prime minister and Finance minister, bringing the necessary experience with him. Now began a tussle between Indira Gandhi and Morarji Desai that would cast a shadow over their relationship for their remaining days. In July 1969, Desai was relieved of the Finance portfolio by the prime minister. Even though he accepted the prerogative of the prime minister to make periodic changes in his or her council of ministers, Desai felt slighted by the action as he had not been consulted before the decision was made. He therefore resigned from his post as the deputy prime minister.

The next milestone in Desai's life, and the political history of the country, was the split in the Congress party in 1969. Desai became a part of the Congress (O), and Indira Gandhi's supporters became his opponents. From a deputy leader of the ruling party, Desai had become a member of the Opposition in Parliament. He returned victorious to Parliament after the general elections of 1971, even though it was a near landslide victory for Indira Gandhi's faction of the Congress, then known as the Congress (R) and later renamed the Congress (I). Following these general elections, when Indira Gandhi's popularity was at its peak after the war with Pakistan which had led to the creation of Bangladesh, the Congress (O), which Desai was part of, became a marginal force in Indian politics.

However, political events were to move fast and furiously after this. In 1975, Desai went on an indefinite fast for elections to be held in the Gujarat Assembly, which had been dissolved. He succeeded in having elections held in June that year. The Congress (O), part of the Janata Front with other opposition parties and independents, secured an absolute majority in the new Gujarat Assembly. Indira Gandhi clearly saw this as a reversal, and following the adverse judgement against her election to the Lok Sabha by the Allahabad high court in the famous case filed by Raj Narain, she declared a state of national Emergency on 26 June 1975. All the opposition leaders, including Desai and Jayaprakash Narayan, were put in jail.

Desai was kept in solitary confinement and only released on 18 January 1977. When elections to the Lok Sabha were announced, Desai threw himself with active enthusiasm into the task of unseating Indira Gandhi's government by democratic means. He played a large role in the resounding victory of the Janata Party in the 1977 general elections, himself being elected to the Lok Sabha from Surat. Unanimously elected leader of the Janata Party in Parliament, Morarji Desai was sworn in as the fifth prime minister of India on 24 March 1977. He was the first prime minister of India who was not a member of the Congress party at the time of taking office.

Some of the memorable achievements of the Desai government, severely challenged by infighting between the different constituents of the Janata Party, were the improvement of relations with Pakistan which had suffered a setback after the 1971 war, and restoring of ties with China. His government cancelled some of the laws passed during Emergency, making it difficult for any future government to impose Emergency and suspend the rights of Indian citizens. Remarkably, Desai is the only leader to have received the highest civilian awards of both India and Pakistan — Bharat Ratna and Nishaan-e-Pakistan respectively.

After Charan Singh withdrew his support from the Janata government in 1979, Desai resigned from office and retired from active politics at the age of eighty-three. He was remarkably fit and alert for his age, even if disillusioned by the political events of the last few years. For the next sixteen years, he lived a quiet life as an ordinary citizen in Mumbai, receiving several honours for being the last great freedom fighter of his generation. Among the factors that his longevity was attributed to, were some unorthodox medical treatments like auto-urine therapy, which he periodically advocated.

In many ways, Desai represented the staunch, fearless and upright figure of the patriotic Indian, untroubled by the more glamorous face of modernity and consumerism.

Chaudhry Charan Singh (1902–1987)

A Farmer at the Helm
Chaudhry Charan Singh

Term of Office: 28 July 1979–14 January 1980

The farmer's horizon is often only the point where his fields meet that of his neighbour. Used to living a life in rhythm with the sun and the sky, the rain and the earth, these men, who play such an important role in the development of our country, were few and far between in public and political life. That is, till one leader changed the city-dweller's perception of farmers and brought rural India firmly into national focus.

Chaudhry Charan Singh, the fifth prime minister of independent India, represented the peasants and farmers of rural India. It is the unwavering hard work and commitment of these men that made our country first self-sufficient in terms of food, and next, a strong economic power backed by strength in agriculture.

Charan Singh belonged to the Jat community. This ethnic community is found in large parts of north India and Pakistan. Believed to be descendants of the original Indo-Aryan or Indo-Scythian tribes of the country, Jats are found among followers of several different faiths – they can be Hindu, Muslim or Sikh. Traditionally farmers, members of this peasant community have also distinguished themselves in military service. The Jat Regiment is one of the oldest regiments of the Indian army, with many decorated officers and soldiers.

Maharaja Nahar Singh of Ballabhgarh in present-day Haryana was a prominent figure in the first struggle for independence in 1857. Leading his forces against the British, he was the uncrowned king of Delhi for four months in 1857 before being sent to the gallows in Chandni Chowk by the British administration that had succeeded in crushing the Indian resistance. It was because of the persecution of Nahar Singh's followers by the British following his execution, that Singh's grandfather moved to Bulandshahr in Uttar Pradesh.

Here, in Noorpur, a town in Meerut district, Singh was born on 23 December 1902. The son of a peasant with relatively little access to the world of letters, Singh was a good student, whose results revealed his application. He graduated in science in 1923, and did his post-graduation from Agra University in 1925. He completed his studies as a lawyer in 1926, and set up practice at Ghaziabad. Like many young lawyers of that time, he was fired by the ideals of India's struggle for independence, and in 1929, he moved to Meerut and joined the Congress.

Married to Gayatri Devi, Singh had four daughters, Satya, Vedvati, Gyanvati and Sharda, and a son, Ajit Singh, who has also been active in the Indian political scene. As one of the idealistic and youthful followers of Mahatma Gandhi in the non-violent struggle, Singh was imprisoned several times by the British government. In 1930 he was sent to jail for six months for contravention of salt laws. He was jailed again for one year in November 1940, and in August 1942 during the Quit India Movement. He was released in November 1943.

His political career can be said to have begun in February 1937, when he was elected from Chhatrauli to the Legislative Assembly of Uttar Pradesh, then known as United Provinces, at the age of thirty-four. As a legislator, he introduced an Agricultural Produce Market Bill in the Assembly in 1938, which reflected his concern for farmers. This Bill was intended to protect the interests of the farmers from sharp practices adopted by traders, and get them a better price for their produce. The Bill was so far-reaching that it was adopted by most states in India, with Punjab being the first state to adopt it in 1940. Singh supported tenant rights, and his early work went against the more established influences within the Congress party, where there was a visibly dominant group of landlords. Singh attempted to draw support for the peasant ownership of land, making the person who tilled the land its rightful owner. He implemented reforms in rural land ownership and taxation whenever he was in power, and prevented tax increases on farmers. His main contribution to Indian politics was to make farmers into an articulate and viable political force. It is for this reason that he is considered to be a leader of farmers.

Singh represented Chhatrauli again in 1946, 1952, 1962 and 1967. His administrative experience gained ground first as a parliamentary secretary in Pandit Govind Ballabh Pant's government in

1946, when he worked in the departments of Revenue, Medical and Public Health, Justice, and Information. Following independence, he became a Cabinet minister in the state of Uttar Pradesh in June 1951, and was given charge of the departments of Justice and Information. He later became minister for Revenue and Agriculture in the Cabinet of Dr Sampurnanand in 1952, and continued to serve in the Uttar Pradesh government till April 1959.

As Revenue minister of Uttar Pradesh, a largely agricultural and densely populated state, Singh was dedicated to enforcing and implementing the provisions of the Zamindari Abolition and Land Reform Act, a law which he himself had principally helped to shape. He believed that no democracy could succeed if its land was held in the hands of a few powerful landlords or zamindars. It was such landlords who were able to run their lands as their private kingdoms in the past. Singh was determined to bring reforms in this area.

However, these ideas and policies brought him into direct confrontation with Jawaharlal Nehru, then the prime minister, who was more influenced by the Soviet model of economic reform. Singh was of the firm opinion that Soviet-style cooperative farms would not succeed in India. Having come from a farmer's family, he forcefully put forward his view that the right of ownership was important to the farmer in remaining a cultivator. Such an open criticism of Prime Minister Nehru's views cost Singh dearly in political terms. In the 1950s, few people questioned Nehru, considered the architect of independent India. It was inevitable that Singh's aggressive voicing of the farmer's cause, and his differences with Nehru, would lead to a different political path. In 1967, he left the Congress and formed his own political party, the Bhartiya Lok Dal. This was also the time when he became the chief minister of Uttar Pradesh, in 1967–68 and again in 1970.

Even though his time as chief minister was relatively short, it was during these stints that Charan Singh began to seriously challenge the united combine of the Brahmin and Bania castes that had dominated Indian politics. Caste has always been one of the factors that influence voters in Indian elections. Singh forged an alliance between the large numbers of Jats and Muslims, thus becoming a force to reckon with in electoral politics. While Jats rallied around him as a natural leader, Singh did not himself emphasise caste in his politics. He believed, rather, in the interests of the rural people as a whole. In addition, his family had been grounded in the teachings of the Arya Samaj, and he retained this more inclusive vision of his countrymen, rather than seeing them as separate castes and communities.

Singh had occupied several positions while in the Uttar Pradesh government, holding the Home, Agriculture and Forests portfolios. In 1966, he took charge of the local self-government department. After the Congress split in 1967, he became the chief minister of Uttar Pradesh for the second time in February 1970 with the support of the Congress party. However, President's Rule was imposed in the state on 2 October 1970, since the split in the Congress and defections by legislators had put the stability of the government in jeopardy.

In 1975, Singh was jailed once again, this time by then prime minister Indira Gandhi, who had declared a state of Emergency and jailed all her political opponents. In the general elections of 1977, all the jailed Opposition leaders succeeded in winning elections and wresting power from the Congress party for the first time since independence. Charan Singh, as a senior leader of the Opposition, was now a part of the government.

The process began with Charan Singh merging his peasant-based Bharatiya Lok Dal with the Janata Party of Morarji Desai in 1977. Singh served as Home minister in 1977–78, and as deputy prime minister in 1979 in the Janata Party government. However, the infighting that developed among the various constituents of the Janata government caused the government to collapse, and later in the same year, Singh became the prime minister of India with the support of the Congress. This was a very vulnerable position to be in, because it was only after great opposition to the policies of Indira Gandhi and the Congress that the Janata government had come to power two years earlier. In becoming a prime minister dependent for parliamentary support from the very party he had been bitterly opposed to, Charan Singh headed a government that was a high-risk proposition.

Sure enough, Indira Gandhi withdrew support from the Charan Singh-led government in a few short weeks. Faced with the prospect of losing the trust vote in Parliament, Charan Singh chose instead to resign. This made him the only prime minister who never faced Parliament, a dubious distinction that eclipsed some of his real achievements.

Charan Singh urged reform in Indian labour laws to make it more competitive in the world economy. As a foreign policy initiative, he opened high-level diplomatic relations with Israel. In his earlier stints in government in Uttar Pradesh, Singh had worked hard to end land-related disparities and injustice. Under his leadership and direction, the Department. Redemption Bill 1939 was formulated and finalised. As chief minister, he brought about the Land Holding Act 1960, which lowered the ceiling on land holdings in an attempt to make them uniform throughout the state. The books he wrote reflected his main concerns, among them *India's Economic Policy – The Gandhian Blueprint, Economic Nightmare of India – Its Cause and Cure* and *Cooperative Farming X-rayed.*

After his resignation as prime minister, Charan Singh never again held public office. He died on 29 May 1987. Fittingly, the memorial spot marking the cremation of this peasant prime minister was named Kisan Ghat.

Rajiv Gandhi (1944–1991)

Destiny's Prime Minister
Rajiv Gandhi

Term of Office: 31 October 1984–1 December 1989

Indira Gandhi's world was shattered by the death of her younger son on 23 June 1980. Sanjay Gandhi, Member of Parliament, and long considered his mother's political heir, had been active in the Youth Congress for several years. During the Emergency, he had wielded extraordinary powers and had collected a number of followers who were anxious to benefit from his proximity to the prime minister. He had also managed to alienate large numbers of the urban poor who were victims of his enforced sterilisation or city beautification drives.

When Sanjay Gandhi died, a grieving Indira Gandhi turned to a son who had always remained out of public view, content to lead the life of an ordinary citizen. This elder son, who was an airline pilot, had steered clear of politics and concentrated instead on having a normal family life with his Italian wife and two children. Rajiv Gandhi, offering what comfort he could to his mother at the time of his brother's death, gave very reluctant consent to contesting for his brother's vacant Lok Sabha seat in 1981. Later, he took over the leadership of the Congress youth wing, self-consciously exchanging his airline pilot hat with the politician's white 'topi' – the headgear his grandfather had once sported.

From 1981 to 1984, although Indira Gandhi groomed her elder son for a political career, she does not seem to have projected him with the same vigour as she had her younger son. And yet, Indira Gandhi had weakened the internal democratic processes within her party so comprehensively, that on the day she was assassinated, Congressmen could look no further to seek a leader to carry the party and country forward than Indira Gandhi's son, who carried the same Nehru–Gandhi brand value.

Rajiv Gandhi, elder son of Indira and Feroze Gandhi and grandson of Jawaharlal Nehru, was born on 20 August 1944 in Bombay. He went to the Doon School in Dehradun, and Cambridge University, where he met Sonia Maino, whom he later married.

Rajiv Gandhi was sworn in as prime minister after a general election in which he rode the huge sympathy wave that followed his mother's assassination. When he became prime minister in 1984, he was forty years old, a young man by the standards of Indian politics. Rajiv Gandhi's ascension to the post of prime minister undoubtedly unleashed hope and cheer among the people. He represented a fresh energy and enthusiasm, and had the kind of ordinary record of a citizen that underlined his 'clean' image, as compared to other politicians. His good looks and easy and approachable manner won him friends not only among India's industrialists, administrators and educated urban people, but abroad as well. With a clear and unhindered majority in Parliament, Rajiv Gandhi had the opportunity to break many traditions and make a real difference to India and Indians.

Rajiv Gandhi did begin to approach the tasks before him with what seemed like a genuine commitment to succeed. He had several challenges before him, with the political and religious violence in Punjab and the Northeast being the most immediate. He also had to reform the structure of the Congress (I), and encourage its cadres, take measures to bring the sluggish economy back on track and reduce tensions with neighbours like Pakistan and Sri Lanka. Several initiatives during this period were noteworthy, like the Rajiv–Longowal Accord in Punjab, which brought about dialogue between the government and the Sikh establishment after a long time. From 1985 to 1987, Rajiv Gandhi showed signs of maturing in his assignment. Economic reforms and incentives to private investors took the form of easier government tax rates and licensing requirements. Corruption, however, remained a worry.

What seems to have let Rajiv Gandhi down was his hurry to bring India into the twenty-first century via technology, without doing enough to tackle the issues that affected the largest section of the people, such as poverty eradication, better housing, infrastructure, education and health care. Rajiv's vision of a modern India made him rely on an inner circle of friends and cronies who pushed for an increase in investments in modern technology. The plus point of this was a virtual revolution in electronics and telecommunications with the country's antiquated telephone systems being completely revamped to meet public demands. Collaboration with the United States and several European governments and corporations increased, and brought in more investment in research and development in electronics and computer software.

Unfortunately, the enduring problems of Indian society, such as poverty and the vast differences in power and wealth between various sections of the people, remained unaffected by many of these measures. Taking more interest in the global role of peacekeeper rather than the internal social and political problems of India, Rajiv undertook to send the Indian Army as the Indian Peace Keeping Force (IPKF) to Sri Lanka in order to help the government there fight LTTE militants agitating for a separate Tamil homeland. This proved disastrous as thousands of Indian soldiers and Tamil militants were killed or wounded.

Better results were seen in India's relations with Pakistan, at the inaugural South Asian Association for Regional Cooperation (SAARC) meet in December 1985. At this meet, both nations began talks that resulted in an agreement in 1986, promising that neither would launch a first strike at the other's nuclear facilities.

Meanwhile, a storm had been stirred up with the ministry of Finance's investigation into tax and foreign exchange evasions by several of India's leading families, including those who had helped Rajiv in election time. At this time, differences began to crop up between Rajiv and his Finance minister, Vishwanath Pratap Singh. V.P. Singh was subsequently removed from the Finance ministry and put in charge of Defence. But this is when the 'Bofors' ghost began to haunt Rajiv Gandhi.

In 1986, India had purchased US$1.3 billion worth of artillery pieces from the Swedish manufacturer A.B. Bofors. Later, reports appeared in the Swedish media alleging that Bofors had won this mammoth export order by bribing Indian politicians and defence personnel. The demand for details of the Bofors deal to be made public acquired a nationwide following. Political opponents alleged that Rajiv Gandhi was somehow connected with the deal through friends like Ottavio Quattrochi, an Italian businessman. V.P. Singh's resignation from the party over Bofors and his subsequent political moves via the Jan Morcha and the Janata Dal further embarrassed Rajiv Gandhi.

Not being able to deliver change in many significant areas, in spite of the best intentions, and becoming tainted with the Bofors brush led to a reduction in the number of seats that Rajiv Gandhi's party won in the 1989 general elections. While the Congress had more seats than any other party, they did not have a majority, or the necessary support from other parties to form a government. Rajiv Gandhi offered outside support to the Chandra Shekhar government which succeeded the government led by V.P. Singh, but withdrew it and caused fresh elections to be called in 1991. It was when he was campaigning for these elections that he was assassinated by a suicide bomber from the LTTE on 21 May 1991 in Sriperumbudur, a small temple town in Tamil Nadu. This assassination was supposedly retaliation for his having sent IPKF forces to Sri Lanka

Rajiv's death shocked and saddened a country that had reason to hope for a better performance from him, should he have lived to have enjoyed a second stint in power. There was every evidence that the time spent out of the prime minister's chair had brought valuable lessons in wisdom and political maturity to someone who had been catapulted into governance before, but was now truly qualified for it.

Vishwanath Pratap Singh (1931–2008)

Zamindar Champion of the Downtrodden
Vishwanath Pratap Singh

Term of Office: 2 December 1989–10 November 1990

The history of Indian society has often had distressing chapters of cruelty and injustice due to social discrimination and economic disparity. The zamindar or landowning classes in north India were the beneficiaries of such injustice and discrimination. Placed on top of the social ladder, they saw their lands as fiefdoms, and the people who worked for them as mere menials.

Into such a landowning family, a son was born who would one day become the prime minister of India and attempt to redress the social and economic inequalities that had bedevilled the lives of his countrymen. Vishwanath Pratap Singh, son of Raja Bahadur Ram Gopal Singh, was born on 25 June 1931 in Allahabad. In his early childhood, he was adopted as the heir of the raja of Manda, a decision that virtually guaranteed him a privileged and pampered life.

However, the character of the young boy so chosen was very different, and his response to the situation, quite extraordinary. He donated large tracts of land to the Bhoodan movement, founded by freedom fighter Vinoba Bhave, to address the problems of economic disparity in the Indian countryside. Vishwanath got volunteer labourers to build a road to Manda, participating in the activity as well. While building a school in Koraon, within the Manda zamindari, he carried bricks on his head and got Vinoba Bhave to lay its foundation stone. Confirming that his involvement in such projects was no mere whim, he continued to teach in the school after it was constructed.

Vishwanath Pratap was educated at Allahabad, Poona and Varanasi universities, and showed leadership qualities and an interest in the role of students in social and political life during this time. On 25 June 1955, he was married to

Sita Kumari from Deogarh in Rajasthan, a place known for its art and paintings. Eventually, his social and political leanings led him to join the Congress party, and he entered local politics in Allahabad in the years when Jawaharlal Nehru was prime minister.

What set V.P. Singh apart from others right from the beginning were his strong principles of personal honesty and morality – not only could he do no wrong, but he could not be seen to be doing any wrong either. Such an upholding of his personal values as well as public perception about them, were qualities that would stay with him throughout his political career and public life.

He first became a member of the Legislative Assembly of Uttar Pradesh in 1969, but it was in 1980, after the Congress came back to power at the Centre, that he took over the reins as chief minister of this large state. When he became chief minister, V.P. Singh vowed to tackle the problem of bandits – the dreaded dacoits who were particularly feared in the rural districts of the southwestern parts of the state. When he was not completely successful, he offered to resign. This set a pattern for the rest of his career as well. His strategy for tackling crises often involved him offering to lay down his own office. By showing the scant importance he attached to clinging on to his chair, V.P. Singh set a moral example that forced the parties involved to review their own stand. Later, as the country's Finance minister and prime minister, such offers from him had a significant impact on political developments.

V.P. Singh's stint at the Centre began in 1984, when Rajiv Gandhi asked him to join the government and appointed him Finance minister. In this ministry V.P. Singh worked towards the gradual relaxation of the licenses for manufacturing, trade, export and import which had kept the Indian economy in tight check during the early years of independence. This was in line with Rajiv Gandhi's own thinking. However, where Rajiv Gandhi and V.P. Singh began to differ was in the extraordinary powers Singh gave to the Enforcement Directorate of the Finance ministry, the wing charged with tracking down tax evaders. This key force conducted a series of high-profile raids on suspected tax evaders of the stature of businessman Dhirubhai Ambani and actor Amitabh Bachchan. Since many such industrialists and celebrities had supported the Congress at the time of election, Rajiv Gandhi was urged to sack a Finance minister who seemed to be burdened with more than an ordinary zeal for honesty and integrity.

As Finance minister, V.P. Singh had also curtailed gold smuggling by reducing gold taxes and giving the police a portion of the smuggled gold that they found. These measures had given him a measure of popularity and acceptance that Rajiv Gandhi found difficult to ignore. He removed V.P. Singh from the Finance ministry and made him Defence minister instead.

In the Defence ministry, V.P. Singh had the opportunity to examine closely the notoriously corrupt process of buying and selling weapons. The country's procurement of arms came under his scrutiny, and soon word began to spread that he had information about the Bofors defence deal that could damage Rajiv Gandhi's reputation. As the rumours began to build into a campaign for information on the deal to be made public, V.P. Singh was dismissed from the Cabinet. He was left with no option other than to resign his membership in both the Congress party and the Lok Sabha.

The next stage of Singh's political career began with the formation of a party called the

Jan Morcha together with Arun Nehru and Arif Mohammad Khan, former Congressmen who were disgruntled with Rajiv Gandhi's leadership. This began to function as an Opposition party even as Singh re-entered the Lok Sabha after winning a tightly contested by-election from Allahabad, where he defeated Anil Shastri, the son of Lal Bahadur Shastri. The Jan Morcha itself was to be a short-lived entity, because on 11 October 1988, Jayaprakash Narayan's birthday, the Jan Morcha, Janata Party, Lok Dal and Congress (O) announced their merger to form the Janata Dal. This united party was to bring together all the splinter groups opposed to the Rajiv Gandhi government, and V.P. Singh was elected its president.

To explore the options of forming a government with the support of regional parties, the Janata Dal came together with the Dravida Munnettra Kazhagam, Telugu Desam Party and Asom Gana Parishad, and formed the National Front. Its convener was V.P. Singh and its president was the TDP's N.T. Rama Rao.

Fighting the 1989 general elections as a unified force, the National Front had the advantage of electoral understandings with parties as diametrically opposed to each other as the

Bharatiya Janata Party and the Communist parties. The National Front thus succeeded in uniting all the political parties opposed to the Congress, and won a simple majority in the elections with its allies. With this simple majority in the Lok Sabha, it decided to form a government. Neither the Communists nor the BJP were part of this government, as both had decided to lend outside support.

While the National Front had won the elections clearly projecting V.P. Singh as a 'clean' alternative to Bofors-tainted Rajiv Gandhi, there were other leaders within the Janata Dal camp who were keen to have the prime minister's post. Among these, Chandra Shekhar posed the biggest threat to Singh, as did Devi Lal, the Jat leader from Haryana. Singh staged a clever political sleight-of-hand that showed that he was capable of cunning machinations in the world of politics. At a National Front meeting in the Central Hall of Parliament on 1 December, he proposed the name of Devi Lal as prime minister. At this point Devi Lal stood up and refused the nomination, and said he would prefer to be an 'elder uncle' to the government, and that Singh should be prime minister. Chandra Shekhar was surprised by this assertion and suspected a secret understanding between Singh and Devi Lal, to which he was not party. He was so infuriated that he refused to serve in the Cabinet. Not having such a prominent rival stepping on his toes within the government was actually an asset to V.P. Singh.

However, notwithstanding such an advantage, Singh held office for slightly less than a year, from 2 December 1989 to 10 November 1990 because of internal squabbling. Although a short one, V.P. Singh's term was not without challenges. Within a few days of his taking office as prime minister, terrorists kidnapped the daughter of his Home minister, Mufti Mohammad Sayeed. In a controversial decision, his government gave in to the demands of the kidnappers – that several terrorists in custody be released. His appointment of Jagmohan Malhotra as the governor of Jammu and Kashmir, under the urging of the BJP, was also criticised after Malhotra ordered army troops to fire on the funeral procession of the unofficial head of Kashmiri Islam, the Mirwaiz.

Singh made a much-publicised visit to the Golden Temple in Amritsar, to ask forgiveness for Operation Bluestar, the commando operation within the Golden Temple that had shaken the

Sikh faith and led to the assassination of Indira Gandhi. This had a positive effect, leading to a reduction of the extremism and militancy in Punjab. V.P. Singh also withdrew the IPKF – the Indian army fighting the LTTE in the jungles of Sri Lanka – which had been sent there during Rajiv Gandhi's tenure.

The most notable decision of Singh's tenure as prime minister was his decision to implement the recommendations of the Mandal Commission which suggested that a fixed quota of all jobs in the public sector be reserved for members of the historically disadvantaged Other Backward Classes or OBCs. Motivated partly by his desire for social justice that he had possessed since childhood, and partly because he wished to consolidate the votes from different castes for the Janata Dal, Singh announced his government's commitment to implement the Mandal Commission's recommendations.

A wave of protests by educated urban youths from the upper castes, who were opposed to further quotas of reservation in education and employment, swept over north India. A young protestor set himself on fire and became the defining image of those troubled times. However, Singh's government was set to fall not because of such public resentment, but because of political vendetta.

The BJP in this period was moving forward with the agitation for a temple to be built on the site of the Babri Masjid in Ayodhya, and the protest took on a new shape with party president, Lal Krishna Advani, touring the northern states on his 'rath yatra'. Singh had Advani arrested on the charges of disturbing the peace and fermenting communal tension before he could complete his tour. An outraged BJP withdrew outside support to Singh's government, forcing him to face a vote of confidence.

V.P. Singh's speech as he faced the vote of confidence was notable for his question to his political opponents. 'What kind of India do you want?' he asked them, reminding them of the harm that could come from the destruction of the Babri Masjid and the tearing of the secular fabric that bound Indian citizens. He also declared that he occupied the high moral ground, as he stood for secularism, and was saving the Babri Masjid at the cost of power. Although he lost the confidence vote 142–346 and his government fell, his personal values, and the public perception that he had remained true to those values, still remained.

V.P. Singh left public life and only re-entered it to make significant statements and interventions. He focused on his poetry and painting, and continued to live according to the high standards he set for himself till his death on 27 November 2008.

Chandra Shekhar (1927–2007)

Padayatri Prime Minister
Chandra Shekhar

Term of Office: 10 November 1990–21 June 1991

Few prime ministers have traversed such a varied journey of ideology and geography, or covered such a vast political terrain, as Chandra Shekhar, India's ninth prime minister, who held office for a short period of seven months. When Chandra Shekhar's government fell in March 1991, because of the withdrawal of 'outside support' by the Congress party, he had been leading a minority government with only sixty MPs and the support of parties as ideologically opposed as the Communists and the Bharatiya Janata Party. Bringing together such disparate elements was a peculiar talent of Chandra Shekhar's personality.

Chandra Shekhar was born Chandra Shekhar Singh into a family of farmers on 1 July 1927 in a village called Ibrahimpatti in Ballia district of Uttar Pradesh.

Chandra Shekhar attended Allahabad University, obtaining his Master's degree in political science in 1950–51. As a young man, he was attracted to the politics and personality of Acharya Narendra Dev, a fiery socialist leader. Under his tutelage, he became known in socialist circles, serving as secretary of the district Praja Socialist Party, Ballia, as well as joint secretary of the Uttar Pradesh state Praja Socialist Party. In 1955–56 he took over as general secretary of the Uttar Pradesh state Praja Socialist Party.

His early stint in Parliament was in the Rajya Sabha, where he was a member from Uttar Pradesh in the period 1962 to 1967. By January 1965, he had joined the Indian National Congress. Here too, he began to be noticed and was elected general secretary of the Congress parliamentary party in 1967. Becoming a spokesman of the younger crop of leaders then in national politics and within the Congress, he founded and edited *Young Indian*, a weekly that was published from Delhi.

Chandra Shekhar often clashed with the powers-that-be within the Congress party due to his fearless questioning of the establishment. This earned him a reputation of being a 'Young Turk'. Since he believed that ideology and social change were more important than personalities in politics, he was attracted to Jayaprakash Narayan and his ideal of peaceful Total Revolution in 1973–75, the days leading up to the Emergency.

When Emergency was declared, Chandra Shekhar was among the very few individuals within the ruling Congress party to be sent to jail under the infamous MISA or Maintenance of Internal Security Act, because of his record of challenging the powers-that-be in the Congress in the previous few years. When he was jailed, he was a member of the Central Election Committee and Working Committee of the Indian National Congress. After his arrest, the publication of *Young Indian* was stopped and was resumed only much later, in 1989.

After Emergency was lifted, Chandra Shekhar left the Congress and became part of the new Janata Party government. He was president of the Janata Party from 1977 to 1988. He also enjoyed a nearly uninterrupted stint in the Lok

Sabha, being elected to India's lower house of Parliament eight times from Ballia in eastern Uttar Pradesh, beginning in 1977. The only election that he lost was in 1984 against Jagganath Chaudhary of Congress (I). Known for abiding by parliamentary conventions during his long stint as a Lok Sabha MP, Chandra Shekhar was honoured with the inaugural Outstanding Parliamentarian Award in 1995.

In 1984, Chandra Shekhar made a significant impression on the national scene when he undertook a padayatra or 'marathon walk' across the country beginning at Kanyakumari and concluding at Rajghat, the resting place of Mahatma Gandhi in New Delhi. This journey, meant to raise awareness about the compelling issues of common people, covered a distance of nearly 4,260 kilometres and took Chandra Shekhar a little more than five months. The response of the people to this exercise made other political leaders quite nervous, notably then prime minister, Indira Gandhi. On the way, Chandra Shekhar established about fifteen Bharat Yatra Centres in various parts of the country, including Kerala, Tamil Nadu, Karnataka, Maharashtra, Madhya Pradesh, Gujarat, Uttar Pradesh and Haryana.

These centres functioned to train social and political workers for grassroots work in different parts of the country.

When V.P. Singh resigned from the post of prime minister, Chandra Shekhar formed a breakaway faction of the Janata Dal called the Samajwadi Janata Party, consisting of sixty-four MPs, and staked a claim to forming a government under his leadership. In order to avoid mid-term elections, the Congress decided to extend outside support to his government, which was also supported by the Communist parties and the BJP.

However, the promised 'outside support' by the Congress was quickly withdrawn, ostensibly because of the charge that the Chandra Shekhar government had been spying on Rajiv Gandhi, the Congress leader at the time. Boycotting Parliament after making this accusation, the Congress party precipitated a delicate political situation wherein Shekhar was prime minister with the loyal support of only about sixty MPs, and the rest shifting their loyalties. Left with little alternative except to resign, he did so while explaining the reasons for his decision in a nationally televised address.

Chandra Shekhar held the office of prime minister for only seven months, and resigned from the post of prime minister on 6 March 1991. However, he remained in office till national elections could be held later that year.

His experiences in jail during the Emergency have been captured in his diary, written in Hindi and published under the title *Meri Jail Diary*. Aspects of his social and political vision can be found in a compilation of his writings called *Dynamics of Social Change*.

Chandra Shekhar died on 3 May 2007 from multiple myeloma, a form of cancer, mourned by his political adversaries as well as his colleagues in the social and political arena.

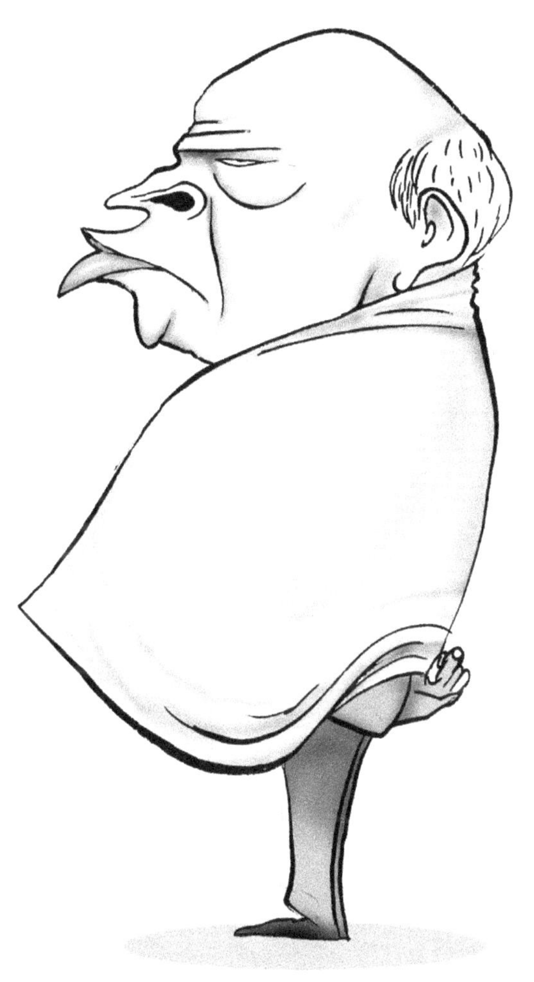

P.V. Narasimha Rao (1921–2004)

Reformist Prime Minister of Modern India
P.V. Narasimha Rao

Term of Office: 21 June 1991–10 May 1996

P.V. Narasimha Rao's five years in office will be remembered for the first completion of a full term by a coalition government in the republic of India, the transition of India from a closed socialist economy to a market-driven one, and the destruction of the Babri Masjid which unleashed communal tensions across the country.

Narasimha Rao was born Pamulaparthi Venkata Narasimha Rao on 28 June 1921 at Vangara village in Karimnagar district of Andhra Pradesh. His father, P. Ranga Rao, was a wealthy Brahmin landowner. Narasimha Rao, known popularly as

PV, showed an early aptitude for languages. He completed his Bachelor's and Master's degrees in law from Osmania University, Hyderabad, and the universities of Mumbai and Nagpur. By the time he completed his education, he could speak thirteen languages, including Urdu, Marathi, Kannada, Hindi, Telugu and English, with the fluency of a native speaker. He would later go on to learn French, Arabic, Spanish and Persian.

Although his parents and family had groomed him for a career as an advocate, they also expected him to oversee their large holdings in agriculture. However, PV had literary interests which found expression in articles supporting the Indian struggle for independence. He joined hands with his cousin Pamulaparthi Sadasiva Rao to edit a Telugu weekly magazine called *Kakatiya Patrika* from 1948 to 1955, which commented on social and political developments. This period also saw the beginning of his political career by his becoming a member of the Indian National Congress.

P.V.N. Rao was a member of the Andhra Pradesh Legislative Assembly for twenty years, from 1957 to 1977, during which period he held many ministerial berths including Law and Information,

Health and Medicine, and Education. In 1971 he became chief minister of Andhra Pradesh and governed the state for a period of two years.

When the Congress party split, Rao stayed with Indira Gandhi. This led to his emergence on the national stage in 1972, wherein he handled several diverse portfolios such as the key ministries of Home, Defence and Foreign Affairs between 1980 and 1984 in the Cabinets of both Indira and Rajiv Gandhi. His capability and administrative experience had drawn so much notice by then that it was widely speculated that he would be in the running for the post of India's president along with Zail Singh in 1982. Most importantly, Rao had remained steadfastly loyal to Indira Gandhi during the Emergency from 1975 to 1977, when she was drawing national and international criticism for stifling all opposition and suppressing democratic rights.

While the ministerial berths he had occupied had made him a figure to reckon with in national politics, he very nearly retired from politics in 1991, due to indifferent health. Rajiv Gandhi's assassination in 1991 led to the search for a leader acceptable to the rank and file of the Congress party. Due to the premium placed on loyalty to the Nehru–Gandhi family within the Congress, only a stalwart like Rao, who had been demonstrably loyal to Indira and Rajiv Gandhi, could hope to lead the party. It was this factor that was largely responsible for his making a political comeback in 1991, leading the Congress and forming a coalition government at the Centre with himself as prime minister, in which a number of parties offered outside support, and the BJP became the largest Opposition party.

Rao had not contested the general elections when he became prime minister, so he had to stand in a by-election to enter Parliament. He was elected from Nandyal in Andhra Pradesh, with a victory margin of five lakh votes – a record victory that has been entered in the *Guinness Book of World Records*. In fact, Narasimha Rao's government set several records: Rao was the first person outside the Nehru–Gandhi family to complete his prime ministerial term, the first prime minister from south India, and also the first from the state of Andhra Pradesh. Rao's Cabinet was notable for having Sharad Pawar, himself a strong contender for the prime minister's post, as Defence minister, and most importantly, a non-political economist, Manmohan Singh, as Finance minister. It was this last choice that would prove significant for India, as Dr Manmohan Singh spearheaded the effort to open up the Indian economy by initiating large-scale reforms in the licensing and regulation of industry and commerce, investment and banking. These sweeping economic changes began to have an immediate effect with growing international investment in India. For the man on the street, the result of such measures was visible in the expansion of products, services and brand names.

Rao's government broke with convention in other areas of governance as well. The Defence budget was increased during his time, when the country was facing the threat of terrorism and insurgency. Terrorism in the state of Punjab was finally defeated during his term. He directed negotiations to secure the release of K. Doraiswamy, an Indian Oil executive, from Kashmiri terrorists who had kidnapped him, and Liviu Radu, a Romanian diplomat posted in New Delhi in October 1991, who was kidnapped by Sikh terrorists. He was also in the prime ministerial seat at the time of the occupation of the Hazratbal holy shrine in Jammu and Kashmir by Pakistan-sponsored terrorists in October 1993, and his government had to deliver a fitting response. Creditably, he was able to bring the occupation to an end without damage to the shrine.

Rao's experience in international affairs showed in his government's successful diplomatic initiatives vis-à-vis Western Europe, the United States and China. In 1992 he brought out in the open India's relations with Israel, and permitted that country to open an embassy in New Delhi. He helped focus international attention on Pakistan's sponsorship of terrorism within India, particularly after the Mumbai blasts of 12 March 1993. Personally visiting Mumbai after the blasts and seeing evidence of Pakistani involvement in their execution, he asked the intelligence agencies of the US, UK and other West European countries to send their experts to Mumbai and examine facts for themselves. Rao succeeded in this mission even though the US exerted itself to undermine India's efforts.

Alongside his political career, Rao's literary accomplishments continued. He published *Sahasra Phan*, a Hindi translation of late Shri Viswanatha Satyanarayana's famous Telugu novel *Veyi Padagalu*. His Telugu translation of Shri Hari Narayan Apte's famous Marathi novel, *Pan*

Lakshat Kon Gheto, was called *Abala Jeevitam* and brought out by the Central Sahitya Akademi. He translated several famous works from Marathi to Telugu and from Telugu to Hindi, and published many articles in different magazines under a pseudonym.

Towards the end of his term, Rao's government was challenged on several counts. He had to face a no-confidence vote in Parliament in 1994, and in 1996, his government was rocked by a corruption scandal wherein he was alleged to have bought the votes of Jharkhand Mukti Morcha (JMM) Members of Parliament in the vote of confidence two years earlier. The 1996 general elections saw the Congress voted out of power, with a considerably reduced number of seats in Parliament. Rao relinquished his prime ministership, bringing down the curtain on one of the most eventful and significant periods in modern Indian history. He retained leadership of the Congress party till late 1996.

When he moved out of the direct public gaze, he published a novel, *The Insider*, which many considered to be his own story. However, he denied any autobiographical connection. The stigma of corruption would prove difficult to shake off as a series of scandals such as the St Kitts forgery case and the Lakhubhai Pathak cheating case continued to dog him, particularly through his association with controversial 'godman' Chandraswami. While he was acquitted of charges in the JMM bribery case in 2002, Rao was not charged, due to lack of evidence, in the other two cases. However, the damage to his reputation had been done.

P.V. Narasimha Rao passed away in December 2004 at the age of eighty-three. One of his quotes actually reveals a lot about the man known for his enigmatic silence on many burning issues: 'Time itself is the solution to all problems.'

Atal Bihari Vajpayee (b. 1924)

Statesman Prime Minister
Atal Bihari Vajpayee

Terms of Office: 16 May 1996–1 June 1996;
19 March 1998–22 May 2004

India's political atmosphere is often vitiated by bitter criticism and personal attacks. Politicians of all hues have lost their standing in the estimation of the people because of their lack of dignity and the way in which they slander each other in public statements. Yet, one prime minister who had a long career of over fifty years as a parliamentarian has managed to have friends and well-wishers from across political parties and camps. He has been the prime minister of the country through three successive elections, like Jawaharlal Nehru. However, his first two terms as prime minister were cut prematurely short by different political circumstances, and only in his third term in office did he govern for nearly five years before calling for premature elections. This veteran parliamentarian prime minister who commanded the respect of all his political friends and foes was Atal Bihari Vajpayee.

Vajpayee was India's prime minister for a mere thirteen days in 1996. At the time, although the Bharatiya Janata Party, the party that Vajpayee represented, had emerged as the single largest party in the Lok Sabha, it was not able to muster the support from other parties needed to win a motion of confidence. Vajpayee resigned and made way for the short-lived governments of I.K. Gujral and H.D. Deve Gowda. When fresh elections were held in 1998, Vajpayee's party was again the single largest party, with a more comfortable majority. He was sworn in as prime minister, and remained so for thirteen months till the AIADMK leader Dr J. Jayalalithaa withdrew support for his government in the Lok Sabha, causing Vajpayee's government to fall once again. No attempt was made to form a government from the same fractured Lok Sabha, since the experiments with I.K Gujral and H.D. Deve Gowda had proved so short-lived. Fresh elections were called in 1999, and this time Vajpayee became prime minister on the strength of his party having the support of several other smaller and regional parties. This alliance became known as the National Democratic Alliance or NDA, and it gave Vajpayee the support he needed to complete a full term in office. He thus remained prime minister till his party lost the next general elections in May 2004.

The main reason why Vajpayee found it so difficult to obtain the support from his political opponents was because he belonged to a party that represents the Hindu nationalist ideology in Indian politics. The Bharatiya Janata Party or BJP, which Vajpayee co-founded in 1980, is a reincarnation of the Bharatiya Jan Sangh (BJS), the party that Vajpayee belonged to till 1977, when it was merged with other parties opposed to Indira Gandhi's rule and the imposition of Emergency. The Jan Sangh derived its ideas and motivation from the Rashriya Swayamsevak Sangh or RSS. The RSS, while maintaining itself as a social service organisation, promotes the idea of a Hindu nation and preaches what it regards as 'true' Hindu values or Hindutva. When the BJP first emerged as the single largest party in Parliament, it was unable to convince other parties to join it because most of them, barring a few regional and religious outfits, pledge to uphold the secular fabric of India.

As India's first non-Congress prime minister, who was also not a socialist of the Ram Manohar Lohia School, Vajpayee brought to the prime minister's office an ideology that was for many years outside the political mainstream in India. However, his popularity and acceptability had a lot to do with his personal qualities. In fact, within the Hindu nationalist fold of the Sangh Parivar, a term that is used to describe the RSS, the BJP and many other sister organisations like the Vishwa Hindu Parishad or VHP, Vajpayee has always been a distinctly moderate voice.

Atal Bihari Vajpayee was born on 25 December 1924 in Gwalior, one among seven siblings. His father was a school teacher called Krishna Bihari Vajpayee, and his mother's name was Krishna Devi. He studied at Gwalior and Kanpur, getting his Master's degree in political science from the DAV College at Kanpur. Later he began studying law, but discontinued it after some time.

Young Vajpayee joined politics as a freedom-fighter during the Quit India Movement of 1942–45. However, his ideological growth was not influenced by Mahatma Gandhi, like many others of his generation. Instead, he found a role model in Shyama Prasad Mukherjee, considered the godfather of modern Hindutva and the founder of the BJS. Vajpayee joined the RSS and became a close follower of Mukherjee.

When Mukherjee went on a fast-unto-death in Kashmir in 1953, Vajpayee was by his side. This fast was to protest the rule that required Indian citizens to carry identity cards in Kashmir; the 'inferior' treatment of Indians in the state; and the special status of Kashmir under the Indian Constitution because it had a Muslim majority. The protest had the effect it sought – the identity card rule was recalled – but the whole exercise had left Mukherjee weak and ill, and his health never recovered. To a young Vajpayee, these were emotional moments. It was following Mukherjee's death that Vajpayee stood for and won his first election to Parliament in 1957.

Atal Bihari Vajpayee was the president of the BJS between 1968 and 1973. His career as a parliamentarian is quite unique. He has been a member of both the Lok Sabha and the Rajya Sabha. He has represented large towns like his home town of Gwalior, and the city of Lucknow. He has won elections to the Lok Sabha nine times and to the Rajya Sabha twice. His popular following has been such that he is the only Indian politician to be elected from four different states and six different constituencies.

Before becoming prime minister, Vajpayee served as the minister for External Affairs in the government of Morarji Desai from March 1977 to July 1979. The in-fighting between the different constituents of the Janata Party led to Vajpayee leaving it in 1980, and becoming one of the founders of the BJP. He has been leader of the BJP parliamentary party between 1980 and 1984, in 1986 and between 1993 and 1996. He was a distinguished Leader of the Opposition in the eleventh Lok Sabha.

His term as minister for External Affairs had several milestones. One was a historic visit to China in 1979, the first attempt to normalise relations with that country since the 1962 Sino-Indian war. Another was a visit to Pakistan, which succeeded in initiating normal dialogue and trade relations that had been suspended since the 1971 Indo-Pak war. Vajpayee also represented India at the Conference on Disarmament at this time, where he defended the national nuclear programme as a necessity for India's security, especially since neighbouring China was already a nuclear power. Notably, it was Indira Gandhi, Vajpayee's bitter political opponent, under whose orders India had carried out its first nuclear explosion at Pokhran. By the time he resigned from the government in 1979, due to the bitter in-fighting between the various constituents of the Janata Party for the post of prime minister, Vajpayee had emerged as a credible and respected statesman and political leader.

In the period leading up to L.K. Advani's 'rath yatra' in 1990, Vajpayee continued as president of the BJP and Leader of the Opposition in Parliament. However, it was clear to all that much more hard-line Hindu nationalists were now calling the shots within the BJP. The rise of the BJP was directly linked to their ability to create a sense of grievance among Hindus, that their religious interests were being ignored by the government. Successive Congress governments had pandered to the interests of Muslims, was the BJP's view, and the 'Ram Janmabhoomi' agitation became a symbol for their disenchantment. This movement, which was led by activists of the VHP and the RSS, sought to build a temple dedicated to the god Rama at the site of the Babri mosque in Ayodhya.

Hindu activists claimed that this mosque had been built by Babar after razing and destroying holy sites around lord Rama's birthplace.

The agitation culminated on 6 December 1992, when hundreds of VHP and BJP activists destroyed the Babri Masjid in Ayodhya. Following this, violence between Hindus and Muslims erupted in many parts of the country, with several getting killed. While the VHP was banned by the government, several leaders, including L.K. Advani, were arrested. Vajpayee's inability to draw support from other political parties was chiefly due to these factors in 1996, when he took the office of prime minister for the first time. However, the very fact that he was called to be prime minister in the first place reflected the BJP's increasing acceptance among voters.

Vajpayee was sworn in as prime minister for the third time on 13 October 1999, this time heading a new coalition government, the National Democratic Alliance. The different terms of Vajpayee's leadership were memorable because of several important developments. One of these was the five underground nuclear weapons tests India conducted in Pokhran, Rajasthan, in May 1998. At that time, Vajpayee's government had been in power for only a month, and the international community was shocked, with protests from the US, Canada, Japan, UK and the European Union, who imposed sanctions on the sale of military equipment and high-tech scientific information, resources and technology to India.

In spite of this, the nuclear tests were largely welcomed within India as people saw them as an important aspect of India's security. Many important economic and infrastructural reforms were introduced by the Vajpayee administration encouraging the private sector and foreign investments; reducing wasteful government spending; giving a fillip to research and development; and privatising public sector undertakings.

Following his earlier efforts as External Affairs minister, Vajpayee began the process of diplomatic efforts to restore peace between India and Pakistan in late 1998 and early 1999. The Delhi–Lahore bus service was inaugurated in February 1999. In spite of such efforts, the nation was witness to the Kargil invasion, when thousands of insurgents and Pakistani soldiers out of uniform infiltrated into the Kashmir Valley and captured control of border hilltops and unmanned border posts.

'Operation Vijay' launched by the Indian army in June 1999 was an operation carried out in extremely cold weather, snow and treacherous terrain at high altitudes. Over 500 Indian soldiers died in this three-month long war.

Vajpayee's next crisis came during his third term as prime minister in December 1999, when an Indian Airlines flight was hijacked and flown via Pakistan to Taliban-ruled Afghanistan. There was intense pressure on the government to yield to the demands of the terrorists, from the relatives of the hijacked passengers. The hijackers' demands included the release of certain imprisoned Kashmiri terrorists, including Masood Azhar, the ideologue of the militant group Harkat-ul-Ansar. Vajpayee's government ultimately gave in, a decision that is undoubtedly viewed as a black mark for them, and Jaswant Singh, the Indian External Affairs minister, flew with the released terrorists to Afghanistan and exchanged them for the passengers.

A positive development was the beginning of construction on the 'Golden Quadrilateral', or National Highway Development Project, which would link the country through international quality roads. Continuing his efforts for peace with Pakistan, Vajpayee succeeded in having

President Pervez Musharraf visit India for talks at Agra. However, these did not lead to any real gains. On the other hand, the government was challenged again by the December 2001 attack on Parliament.

With the terrorist threat looming large, the country was pushed further into gloom when a group of Hindu pilgrims returning from Ayodhya were burnt in the Sabarmati Express at Godhra station in February 2002. The rumour spread that the fire was caused by Muslims, and this led to a wave of reactionary attacks in Gujarat which claimed the lives of thousands of Muslims. Gujarat's BJP government, led by Narendra Modi, and the police were widely perceived to have aided and abetted the rioters who burnt and destroyed Muslim homes and families.

In spite of all this, in late 2003, it appeared as if the BJP would return to power. The BJP wooed the rising urban middle-class and the youth with their 'India Shining' advertising campaign. Their defeat and the swearing in of the Manmohan Singh UPA government in 2004 spelt Vajpayee's gradual retirement from public life. In December 2005, Vajpayee announced his retirement, declaring that he would not participate in the next general election. Since then, his failing health has precluded him from being an active commentator on issues of national importance.

Apart from being a politician, Atal Bihari Vajpayee has been an editor, writer and poet. He has edited magazines and newspapers, and published several works including collections of his speeches in Parliament and his poetry.

Vajpayee received India's second highest civilian honour, the Padma Vibhushan in 1992. In 1994, he was conferred the Lokmanya Tilak Puruskar and the Pandit Govind Ballabh Pant Award for the Best Parliamentarian, both in 1994. Kanpur University honoured him with an Honorary Doctorate of Philosophy in 1993.

H.D. Deve Gowda (b. 1933)

Son of the Soil
H.D. Deve Gowda

Term of Office: 1 June 1996–21 April 1997

Immediately after the 1975–77 Emergency, all parties opposed to Indira Gandhi and the Congress united to form the Janata Party and a new government. Later this government broke up into factions. The BJP was born in 1980, and other parties kept forming newer groupings and taking on new names.

One such grouping of different parties was the United Front, which came into existence in 1996 after Prime Minister Atal Bihari Vajpayee resigned before facing the vote of no-confidence that would have removed his government from office. Reluctant to face elections only weeks after the last one, parties like the Janata Dal, the Samajwadi Party, both the Communist parties and other regional parties got together to form the United Front. The question of who would be the prime minister was a tricky one: in the past, non-Congress governments at the Centre had fallen on just this contentious issue. The United Front discussed the issue for several days and one name came up, of a politician from a southern state, who was not then much known or seen outside his home state. After he had taken over the reins of the United Front government of 1996, people had a chance to know Haradanahalli Dodde Deve Gowda or H.D. Deve Gowda.

H.D. Deve Gowda was born on 18 May 1933 in Haradanahalli village of Holenarsipura taluk in the Hassan district of Karnataka. His parents were simple agriculturists. Deve Gowda earned a diploma in Civil Engineering and became a contractor executing minor civil and public works jobs. His interest in active politics began at the age of twenty. It is at this time that he joined the Congress party, remaining a member till 1962.

Deve Gowda's public life began on a small scale. He earned himself a good reputation and popularity by serving as president of the Anjaneya Co-operative Society and later as a member of the Taluk Development Board, Holenarasipura. He entered the electoral fray at the age of twenty-eight as an Independent. His successful showing in the Karnataka Legislative Assembly in 1962 was due to the fact that he was an effective speaker on the floor of the Assembly, and appreciated by one and all, including his seniors. Subsequently he successfully contested Assembly elections from the Holenarasipura constituency for three consecutive terms from 1967 to 1983. During this long stint in the Karnataka Assembly, it was his role as the Leader of the Opposition in the Assembly, from March 1972 to March 1976 and November 1976 to December 1977, that won him special recognition.

Deve Gowda served as the minister of Public Works and Irrigation of Karnataka, a portfolio close to his heart and experience. As Irrigation minister, he commissioned many projects. In 1987 he resigned from the government protesting against insufficient allocation of funds for irrigation.

Deve Gowda had been in politics both as an Independent and a Congressman. He was a member of the Congress when the party split in 1969, at which time he had joined the wing that was opposed to Prime Minister Indira Gandhi. In 1975, this old rivalry was revived when he was jailed for eighteen months as an opponent of Indira Gandhi's government and the imposition of Emergency.

Using his prison term as an opportunity to learn and grow, Deve Gowda read exhaustively and closely interacted and discussed national affairs with other stalwarts of Indian politics who were jailed along with him. This period of the Emergency actually helped build his personality and perspective on national matters. This reflected in his subsequent political actions and decisions when he became known as a senior leader of the Janata Party, and later the Janata Dal.

Deve Gowda was the president of the Karnataka state Janata Party twice and president of the state Janata Dal in 1994. In fact, the rise of the Janata Dal in Karnataka in 1994 was largely attributed to him. The Janata Dal Legislative Party elected him their leader and he assumed office on 11 December 1994 as the fourteenth chief minister of Karnataka. It was after this that he contested elections from Ramanagar Assembly constituency and won by a thumping majority, proving he was a popular choice as chief minister.

Deve Gowda's administrative acumen and governing skills were tested in his capacity as chief minister. His own experience of politics as well as life at the grassroots level stood him in good stead in addressing the problems of his state. One of the crises he was faced with was the sensitive issue of an Idgah Maidan at Hubli, which had become the centre of a controversy regarding its ownership. Deve Gowda successfully brought about a peaceful solution to the problem. His other achievements during this period included foreign tours to Europe, the Middle East and Singapore, which succeeded in bringing in much-needed foreign investment to Karnataka.

H.D. Deve Gowda was propelled to prime ministership by a series of political manoeuvres, chiefly because the United Front had too many prime ministerial candidates, and his name was a comparatively neutral choice. He liked to refer to his humble beginnings by referring to himself as a 'son of the soil', a tag that stuck to him and was doubtless intended to attract large sections of poor and rural voters. Having tasted electoral defeat and humiliation as well as victory in his long political career, Deve Gowda got the post of prime minister due to a combination of political compulsions and his personal style, which has always been low-profile, but highly effective.

Deve Gowda resigned as chief minister of Karnataka on 30 May 1996 to be sworn in as the eleventh prime minister. The Deve Gowda government collapsed in 1997 due to the withdrawal of support by the Congress, which once again proved to be the destabilising factor, just as in the case of Chandra Shekhar and Charan Singh. However, Deve Gowda's occupation of the post of prime minister proved that there is space for an alternative vision in contemporary Indian politics.

I.K. Gujral (b. 1919)

Diplomat Prime Minister
I.K. Gujral

Term of Office: 21 April 1997–28 November 1997

Being the prime minister of a large and diverse country like India requires a person to possess exceptional skills in dealing with people and sorting out conflicts. Diplomats and ambassadors are naturally equipped for such situations – their entire training helps them to successfully reconcile the differing interests of countries. India has had one such prime minister, whose time in office capped a considerable career as a minister for External Affairs and Information and Broadcasting. The tumultuous period that his government had to oversee tested the mettle of this distinguished prime minister.

Inder Kumar Gujral was sworn into office on 21 April 1997. He was born in undivided Punjab, before the partition of India, in a town called Jhelum on 4 December 1919. His parents, Avtar Narain Gujral and Pushpa Gujral, were both active in the freedom movement. Influenced by their passion and patriotism, Gujral himself was arrested in 1931 at the tender age of eleven, for organising young children in his Jhelum town to protest against the British. At the time, the police gave him a severe beating, but the experience would not deter the young patriot. In 1942, he was jailed again during the Quit India Movement.

Educated in Lahore, Gujral enjoyed prominence in student bodies such as the Lahore Students' Union and the Punjab Students' Federation of which he was the president and general secretary, respectively. He was married to Shiela, a poet and writer, on 26 May 1945. Heading naturally for a career in the Congress after his background in the freedom struggle, Gujral became a Member of Parliament in 1964 and remained so till 1976.

I.K. Gujral was minister of Information and Broadcasting in Indira Gandhi's government. In June 1975, after the proclamation of the Emergency, he was believed to have developed some differences with Sanjay Gandhi about the coverage of the latter's political rallies on Doordarshan, then the only television channel. Many believe that it was these differences that led to him being replaced by V.C. Shukla as Information and Broadcasting minister. At the time, Gujral had stood firm because he did not want to be seen taking orders from Sanjay, who did not hold any post of Constitutional authority.

When Indira Gandhi returned to power in 1980, she appointed Gujral the Ambassador to Russia. However, by the mid-1980s, Gujral's relationship with Indira Gandhi and the Congress she represented had soured sufficiently for him to leave the Congress and join the Janata Dal, a party with mainly socialist leanings and regional bases. In the 1989 elections, Gujral fought the elections and was elected from Jalandhar, Punjab.

Following this victory, he became the minister of External Affairs in the Cabinet headed by Prime Minister V.P. Singh. One of the controversies that erupted at this time was the hug he was seen to have shared with Saddam Hussein, as India's representative. It was sometime after this that Iraq's invasion of Kuwait had led to the first US–Iraq war in 1991. Gujral had to use every bit of his diplomatic acumen to deal with the fallout from this war. He was also in the epicentre of a crisis when the daughter of the then Home minister, Mufti Mohammed Sayeed, was kidnapped by JKLF militants in Kashmir. Prime Minister V.P. Singh sent him to Srinagar to negotiate with the kidnappers for the release of Rubaiya Sayeed.

Mid-term elections were called in 1991, and Gujral contested from Patna, against Janata Dal (S) candidate and then Finance minister Yashwant Sinha. This election was countermanded following complaints of large-scale irregularities in the election process. By 1992, Gujral had been elected to the Rajya Sabha and he remained a key Janata Dal leader over the next few years.

In the 1996 general elections, a United Front government came to power at the centre, under Prime Minister H.D. Deve Gowda. This was a coalition government, dependent on the Congress for outside support. I.K. Gujral was minister for External Affairs under this government as well. It was at this time that he propounded a set of measures for improving relations with neighbouring countries, believing this to be an important part of India's foreign policy. These points became known as the 'Gujral Doctrine'.

The Deve Gowda government collapsed in 1997 after the Congress withdrew support. Negotiations between the United Front and the Congress led to the formation of a new United Front government, headed by a new leader. This leader was I.K. Gujral, who was acceptable to the Congress as well as the United Front. The two parties had arrived at this compromise in order to avoid another mid-term election. While pledging support to this government, the Congress asked that some issues that had caused them concern should be addressed – that they be consulted on important policy matters.

When I.K. Gujral took over as prime minister on 21 April 1997, he was in some aspects inheriting a legacy of bitterness and mistrust between the Congress and the United Front. In spite of this, he was able to maintain good relations with the Congress. When a crisis did arrive for his government, it came from another quarter. The CBI approached the then governor of Bihar, A.R. Kidwai, for permission to prosecute the Bihar chief minister Laloo Prasad Yadav in a corruption case related to the purchase of fodder for cattle. Yadav was a member of the Janata Dal, the party to which Prime Minister Gujral belonged.

When Governer Kidwai granted permission to the CBI for this prosecution, the demand for Yadav's resignation became a huge outcry among all political parties. Faced with this, Gujral asked Yadav to step down, but did not initiate any action against his government. In fact, a while later, when he transferred the CBI director Joginder Singh, who was investigating the case against Laloo Yadav, it began to be considered as an attempt on the part of the prime minister to protect his party colleague. Laloo Prasad Yadav's position in the Janata Dal was becoming increasingly difficult. Realising this, he left the party and formed his own party, the Rashtriya Janata Dal (RJD), on 3 July 1997. This had an impact on Parliament. Out of the forty-five Janata Dal MPs at the time, seventeen left the party and joined the RJD. However, there was no immediate threat to the Gujral government as these rebel MPs continued to remain in the United Front.

Gujral stayed in office for over eleven months, including three months as caretaker prime minister. Political instability marked his term and he had to weather several storms. One crisis arose due to his government recommending the dismissal of the BJP government headed by Kalyan Singh in Uttar Pradesh. This recommendation was sent back by President K.R. Narayanan and also struck down by a decision of the Allahabad high court.

Finally, early November 1997 saw parts of the interim report of the Jain Commission, inquiring into the conspiracy behind Rajiv Gandhi's assassination, appearing in the press. By these reports, the Jain Commission had indicted the political party Dravid Munnetra Kazhagam or DMK for supporting the LTTE, which was responsible for Rajiv Gandhi's assassination. There were DMK ministers in the Union Cabinet of the government headed by Gujral and the Congress began pressurising the government to drop them. Letters on this topic were exchanged between then Congress president Sitaram Kesri and Prime Minister Gujral. When Gujral refused to toe the Congress line, the party withdrew support to his government on 28 November 1997. Following this, Gujral resigned as prime minister, and mid-term elections were called shortly thereafter.

While Prime Minister Gujral's term was marred by political instability, he can take credit for some significant initiatives, such as the improvement of relations with Pakistan. He was also fortunate to be in office when the country celebrated fifty years of independence. For a child freedom-fighter like him, that must have been sweet indeed.

Manmohan Singh (b. 1932)

Economist Prime Minister
Manmohan Singh

Term of Office: 22 May 2004–till date

D r Manmohan Singh became the prime minister of India after a brilliant career as an economist. As a young man, he worked for the International Monetary Fund or IMF, a United Nations institution. From 1982 to 1985, he was the governor of the Reserve Bank of India, and later, in P.V. Narasimha Rao's government, he served as Finance minister from 1991 to 1996. It is during this stint that he was credited with initiating many of the policies that helped change India from a controlled economy to a more open one, in tune with the rest of the world. The measures he took to ensure this included gradually dismantling the process of licenses and permits that governed every aspect of manufacturing and trade in the country, allowing more Foreign Direct Investment into industry, and beginning the process of the privatisation of public sector companies.

His leading role in the Congress government of Narasimha Rao led to him becoming the Leader of the Opposition in the Rajya Sabha from March 1998 to May 2004, when there was a BJP government at the Centre.

The formidable respect and reputation that Manmohan Singh enjoys at home and abroad, was partly shaped by his academic prowess. He was born on 26 September 1932 in Gah, in West Punjab, now in the Chakwal district of Pakistan. He studied economics at the undergraduate and post-graduate level first at the Punjab University in Chandigarh from 1950 to 1954 and then at St John's College in Cambridge University. He earned his PhD in 1962 from Nuffield College, Oxford University. In fact, a PhD scholarship at St John's College and Cambridge University is named after him.

Such an impeccable academic record at some of the best institutions in the world and a personality that has consistently been seen as dignified and full of integrity meant that Manmohan Singh has always been a favourite of the educated upper classes in India. However, political success in our country often depends on a close interaction with life and people at the grassroots level. This could be one of the reasons why Manmohan Singh lost an election to enter the Lok Sabha in 1999 from the South Delhi constituency. Continuing to be a Rajya Sabha member after being elected in 2001 and 2007, he was awarded the Outstanding Parliamentarian Award in 2002. Manmohan Singh is the only prime minister never to have been elected to the Lok Sabha.

Manmohan Singh became prime minister of the country in unusual circumstances. The Congress had emerged as the single largest party after the general elections of May 2004, and was supported by other parties who formed the United Progressive Alliance or UPA. Since Rajiv Gandhi's wife Sonia Gandhi was the leader of the Congress party, it was expected that she would become the prime minister. But her foreign origins was an issue that had always been raised by the Congress' political opponents. It was in this situation that Sonia Gandhi called upon Manmohan Singh, who had always been above political manipulations and enjoyed a completely clean image among the public, to become the prime minister. Manmohan Singh was sworn in on 22 May 2004.

Although Manmohan Singh's career has had many significant milestones, including work as a professor of economics, there is no doubt that the role he played in restructuring India's economy as Narasimha Rao's Finance minister from 1991 to 1996 was a very important one. When Singh initiated the policy of economic liberalisation in order to open the nation to Foreign Direct Investment, there was an acute balance-of-payments crisis. This meant that the Indian government, which was without sufficient reserves to meet its payment obligations, had begun preparations to mortgage its gold reserves to the Bank of England in order to obtain the cash reserves needed to run the country.

It was Manmohan Singh's shrewd understanding of India and his fine knowledge of the interplay of economic factors that led to a turnaround of the Indian economy in the 1990s. India has never looked back since. When Manmohan Singh became prime minister, many felt that he would hold the Finance portfolio himself, since there was no one better qualified than him to do so. However, he entrusted the job to P. Chidambaram.

As prime minister, Manmohan Singh concentrated on reducing the fiscal deficit, providing debt-relief to poor farmers, extending social programmes and advancing the pro-industry economic and tax policies that have boosted the Indian economy since 2002. The important legislations relating to a national guarantee of rural employment and the Right to Information were passed by Parliament in 2005 under Singh's government. Some of these measures have borne fruit, while others have been the source of bitter criticism.

On the diplomatic front, he continued to engage in talks with Pakistan. The warm personal relations he enjoyed with George Bush, president of the United States, have brought him both bouquets and brickbats. This is because this relationship was seen as the source of his government's pushing the Indo–US Civilian Nuclear Agreement between India and the United States. Manmohan Singh's commitment to the Indo–US Nuclear deal was tested in Parliament on 22 July 2008, when his government faced a confidence vote in the Lok Sabha. The vote had become necessary after the Left Front parties had withdrawn their support for the government on the issue of India approaching the International Atomic Energy Agency (IAEA) to push through the Indo–US nuclear deal. Prime Minister Manmohan Singh proved his majority, with the UPA winning the trust vote 275-256. However, this occasion was marked forever in public memory with three BJP MPs waving bundles of cash amounting to Rs 3 crore, within the Lok Sabha, alleging that the votes in support of the government had been bought. The matter was subsequently taken up for investigation by Speaker Somnath Chatterjee and the New Delhi police.

While the political wrangling and bickering that occurred before and after the 22 July trust vote did, for the first time, dent Manmohan Singh's image as a clean politician, the subsequent waiver that India has been able to obtain from the NSG or Nuclear Suppliers Group countries has vindicated his government's diplomacy and stand on international relations. Under this waiver, India does not need to sign the anti-nuclear proliferation treaties drawn up by the US and other nuclear weapon producing countries, and can seek to buy material for the peaceful use of nuclear technology from any of them.

In many ways, this breakthrough on the international arena expressed Manmohan Singh's style of working — quietly, intensely working towards the goals one is committed to fulfilling. While many had not hesitated to call him Sonia Gandhi's yes-man, a kind of proxy prime minister when he first took office, his subsequent stewardship has proved them wrong.

In the last year and a half of his term, Manmohan Singh's leadership has been increasingly faced with the destruction and death caused by terrorist attacks. Bomb blasts at Jaipur, Hyderabad, Bengaluru, Surat and Malegaon have been attributed to domestic terror groups. But the full horror of international terror was seen in the attacks on Mumbai on 26 November 2008, wherein more than two hundred people lost their lives. On the floor of Parliament, on 11 December 2008, Singh reiterated his government's resolve to fight terror with the utmost vigilance. In the last months of his term, his administration can be seen to be engaged in reviewing national security, garnering international support for India's fight against terror and trying to heal the feelings of citizens who have been stunned by the scale of the violence against them.